MW01488932

Never Say Buy,
Never Say Sell

by

Christopher Fielder

Bloomington, IN Milton Keynes, UK

authorHOUSE

AuthorHouse™
1663 Liberty Drive, Suite 200
Bloomington, IN 47403
www.authorhouse.com
Phone: 1-800-839-8640

AuthorHouse™ UK Ltd.
500 Avebury Boulevard
Central Milton Keynes, MK9 2BE
www.authorhouse.co.uk
Phone: 08001974150

© 2006 Christopher Fielder. All rights reserved.

No part of this book may be reproduced, stored in
a retrieval system, or transmitted by any means
without the written permission of the author.

First published by AuthorHouse 3/30/2006

ISBN: 1-4259-1875-1 (sc)

Printed in the United States of America
Bloomington, Indiana

This book is printed on acid-free paper.

Contents

Dedication

I can do all things through Christ who strengthens me.

This book is dedicated to the support of my family and friends who have always stood beside me. My wife MaShon has always believed in me and given me the support to succeed.

Preface: What is "Sales"?

Webster defines sales as: **1**: the act of selling; *specifically*: the transfer of ownership of and title to property from one person to another for a price **2 a :** opportunity of selling or being sold **: b :** distribution by selling.

I want to look at the #2 definition "opportunity of selling or being sold". If you look at selling as an opportunity you will become much better at your task at hand. This book is designed to help any salesperson at any level. I started a sales career very early in life at the age of twenty-one. Directly out of college I entered the sales force as an Account Executive with the second largest Music store retailer in the state of Texas. I will never forget the first day on the job; I was starting a career in sales and did not even know it at that time. I want to discuss what I have learned along the way and how it has helped me to become successful in my career. I will show you the basic "tricks" that I wish I would have known when I started. You will undertake the sales strategy from a beginner level to an advanced level with more years in the field than I have. I will bring you a chance to review lost thoughts and ideas you may have once used but forgot.

To quote one of my mentors: "No magic here...just do the common things uncommonly well" Thomas Harmon. Selling is not magic it is just a way of thinking and correct presentation skills. One of the greatest salespeople was the late Elvis Presley. What you say, I never knew that Elvis sold anything? If you remember nothing else about this book other than this please remember *that selling is all about presentation and selling yourself first.* I keep a picture of Elvis up at my desk at all times to help me remember this. He sold himself through a series steps. He may not have even known this is what he was doing but it is what happened to make him the "King". The product may not have been the best but his presentation and the fact that he sold himself first and his music (or product) second is what made him great. He used a sales technique that we refer to as C.A.K.E. I will go into this a lot in chapter one.

When you walk into a room, send an e-mail, or make the call for a sales appointment make sure you are going in to sell yourself first. People will buy from you just because they like you. Elvis may not have been the best singer but he sold himself and people liked him. He made it as easy as C.A.K.E.

Remember someone is going to get sold. The question is whether it will be you or the customer and to what extent. Hopefully this book will help you to be the one doing the selling. Happy reading and God Bless!

Chapter 1
Concepts

Never say buy, never say sell! I remember the very first sales call I made. I was 21 years old and on my first job out of college. My new boss set me up to travel about 200 miles to a little school in central Texas. I had never made a true sales call in my life. I was as green as a newly mowed pasture. Sure everyone is a salesperson in some form or another. Whether it is trying to sell your parents on letting you stay up at night or the lemonade stand on the corner when you were young. We all sell, whether you succeed at it as a living depends on the understanding of how to sell correctly. Remember someone is going to get sold. Is it you or the customer?

I walked into the band hall to meet with a gentleman named Guy Birdwell. Mr. Birdwell I found out is one of the best sales people I have ever met. My boss at that time was probably the other. He had mastered the presentation and authority concept of sales to a professional level.

Guy and I spent about two hours together that day sitting around and discussing sales. The first thing he asked me was my sales background. Since I really did not have a background I was happy he liked me and decided to help me in my career. The first pointer Guy told me was "never say buy and never say sell". He left it up to me to really understand the underlying meaning of this phrase but it continues to be the backbone of my sales philosophy. It was very obvious who was getting sold and it was not the customer. Guy got every good deal and closing tool out of me that he could. I think I even bought him lunch that day bringing my net sales to Goldthwaite High School as a negative $20.

I learned several things that day and have never forgotten my role when I walk into a sales call. Guy and I have remained friends over the years and he will continue to be one of the first mentors in my sales adventure. Guy continued to help me out whenever I needed it. We made several deals and his approach was a simple one. As long as you are happy, made money, and the customer is happy with the sale than it is a good one.

Those words of "never say buy and never say sell" have been a great help and better understanding to what and how I was to accomplish a career in sales for the rest of my life. When I was self-employed and not really in the sales field, I continued to grow in my ability because of this sales concept. I ultimately achieved the goals that I set out to complete.

"Never say buy, never say sell"

Why was and is this phrase so important? I quickly found out that people do not want to "buy" anything and never want to be "sold". In chapter 2 we will discuss more on why people buy or sell. Customers do not like to buy anything; they want to purchase or acquire an item for a certain purpose or price. Buying indicates that the customer has had to put something out of pocket. We all know that this is really what buying is but it can be reflected in a more positive way if you will use the correct phrase. Would you purchase anything from a salesperson that came up to you on the car lot or in a retail store and ask you "Do you want to buy this item?" or "Looking to buy a car today". What is the response you hear the most? "NO! I do not want to buy anything or I am just looking around. You have started the sale on a negative note and the customer is already on the defensive. You can see by this example how simple phrasing of your "pitch" can greatly help your close rate and make you a better salesperson.

The first thing I always do is to try to take the concept of buying and selling out of the transaction. I like to use phrases like "Mr. Customer, I would like to show you something that you may have never seen before, is that ok with you?" What has just happened here? I have asked for the right to give my sales pitch hopefully without the customer understanding what I am going to do. This type of phrase has also worked great for me because it stirs up an interest of what I have to show the customer. It does not matter what your product is or whether you are selling face to face or over the phone. Try this approach and see what happens. After you have permission to continue, try to show the customer something different in a benefit to your product. Show the customer something that they have never seen before---your presentation. In Chapter 3 we will review the structure of the proper sales call and closes.

I have come to my own conclusion that has no statistical background. I believe that sales are about 85% emotion, 10% financial and 5% true need. This can vary greatly depending on what your product is. If you sell cars this usually fits well, however if office supplies is your product you might reverse the need and financial aspect. The end result is always the same. There is a great amount of emotions in what people purchase and if they like you they will buy from you.

If you get the opportunity to deal with a relationship type of sales this is a little different because you will be dealing with the same customers over and over again. This was the case with my first sales job. I not only worked with the same customers over and over again I also dealt with some of my friends before I was in this business. This is good and bad. There are direct advantages in working with the same customer on a repeat basis. One of these is that the customer will know what to expect from you and what you can expect from the customer. The other is that if you ever mess up on the call it could cost you in the long run. You are counting on this repeat business to succeed.

I had a little game I was able to play with my customers that they learned to like. Every week I went out on a sales call and visited each one of my protected accounts of around 30 customers. I always had my sales tool with me. It was called the "item of the week" and my customers learned to expect it. I would never go on a call without something to sell or present. This is important and it is a different aspect if you specialize in customer service the way we did at the music store. It is very easy to become an order taker. If you sell office supplies, liquor to stores, or feed to farmers don't ever go on a call without an "item of the week".

I had one customer as soon as I would walk in the door the first thing out of his mouth was "Ok, show me the "item of the week" so we can get onto business". This may sound negative but actually it is a very positive statement. The customer just gave me permission to make a presentation on whatever subject I wanted. I always had a new or old item to show. It is not the item; it could be something as small as new color paper or sale on widgets or the latest and greatest bar glasses. The point is never go on a call without something that the customer may not have seen. Although a crude approach sometimes my pitch would be "let me show you my item of the week, I am not sure if you knew we had these" sometimes I would make up an item. I recall a time when a customer had placed an order for a cymbal stand, no cymbal they already had this. The stand price was $74.95. When I went to the account to deliver the stand I had four different examples of cymbals with me. The approach was why would someone ever purchase a new stand without a new cymbal and the sales pitch was to ask "What type of these four cymbals would you like to go with your new stand?" needless to say I sold the $200 cymbal to go with the $75 stand. You can achieve this with a variety of products. Use your imagination, just remember to always have your item of the week and never say "would you like to buy my item of the week?"

Before I started my new sales job I was teaching a class with my former band director Don Thoede. Don is one of my best friends and another mentor in my life. When Don heard that I was going into sales and especially into the music sales he got excited. Don always has words of wisdom for me and rightfully so as he is one of the most successful people I know in his field and has dealt with probably over 20 different music salespeople in his 25+ years as a band director. Don has seen great music stores with super salespeople and he has seen some of the worst along with asking some never to come back to his band hall. So when Don had something to say to me about music or the business of music I always listened.

What were Don's words of wisdom for the young person just starting out? Well you could apply this to any sales job but I have never forgot those word, he said "Chris, the best thing I can tell you about your new job is this, don't ever tell a customer that you are going to do something unless you intend to do it and if you don't know the answer to a question let the customer know that you don't know the answer but that you will find out what the answer is. If you stick to this you will always have a job and always be respected in your field." I always tried to live by this as one of my top rules. It has gotten me a long way. Although simple it carries a lot of weight with me and is always at the back of my mind when a customer asks questions about timeframe or how I can help.

If a customer asks how long it will take to get my car fixed or how long it will be before my computer will be delivered, tell them the truth. "Mr. Customer, it will take six hours to have your car fixed." You will come across as a much more reputable person to deal with if you can tell the truth rather than state it will take about two hours knowing all well there is no way you will have it done in two hours. Treat every customer like they are coming back to you the next time they need a service or product you provide. If you can build loyalty among your customers they will help you with your job as you become closer to them. When I was on the road I always knew when a competitor had been to my account because the customer would tell me so. I had a strong reputation with them and they understood that I was paid on a commission basis. Try to make the customer feel the same respect. I would often share information I might know about their competition or something about a contest they may be involved in. This type of loyalty involved into a great working relationship and a great deal of return business.

To recap: never say buy and never say sell, never tell a customer you are going to do something unless you can and intend to do it. Be loyal to your customers and expect your customers to be loyal to you and make sure that you have your "item of the week" with you at all times.

The Way Elvis Sold

As I mentioned in the preface, I keep a picture of Elvis up in my office or on my desk or somewhere I can see it when I am working on a presentation. Did Elvis have a selling system? Maybe or maybe not but he did have a great way of selling himself first. It has been stated that the first minute of a sales call whether in person or over the phone will determine how the call will go. Whether you will close the business or not you will never get the opportunity to make a first impression a second time. Let's examine the picture of Elvis. You will recall the picture in your mind. Elvis is in his mid 30's in the white jumpsuit from one of his live performances. He is slim with a smile on his face. His suit is perfect and he looks great. You can tell that he is enjoying what he is doing and is confident in his presentation and with himself. The moment Elvis walks on stage you know he means business. He sells himself first. I am one of the biggest Elvis fans ever but I also realize that Elvis was not the best singer or actor. He made it due to his ability to sell.

There is a lot we can learn from the way Elvis sold. When you walk into a sales call are you prepared? Is your suit or shirt pressed? Are your shoes shined, have you watched your weight? Are you clean and orderly? Are you ready for the presentation? Do you look like you enjoy what you are doing or do you look like you are just going through the motions and have to be there? Let me ask, if your competition was making a presentation after you, who would have the best information? Who would have the best ability to close the sale? It better be you. Do you think that anyone would ever want to follow an Elvis concert or be the next person to perform directly after him? Elvis was the King and presented himself in this manner. Elvis was in most cases the only performer for the night. I rarely recall anyone opening up for him and I know that after his very first performances he never opened up for anyone else. He made sure that the attention was on him.

The other great thing that Elvis did in selling himself was he presented himself as the authority figure. When you go to the doctor and he or she looks at you and tells you to stick out your tongue and get on the table what do you do? You stick out your tongue and get on the table. Why? This is a person who you may have never been to or seen before. You do it because the doctor has portrayed himself or herself as the authority figure. This is what you have to do in the sales field. If you are making a recommendation about what type of paper to use in your copier or what type of car battery will work best for your car, you must portray yourself as the professional. My customers always believed when I brought them my item of the week it was because I knew more about that item than they did. I was there solution doctor. I also made sure that I did know everything that I could about the product so I did not get caught off guard. I had a business partner once whom I did not get much out of but he did have one thing I thought worked well. Never pay someone for advice and then don't take it. What exactly does this mean? Well if you have your car in the shop or a salesman at your door that you think you may purchase from and you need a recommendation, listen to it carefully. You are essentially paying for the advice. Don't pay for their advice and then not take it. If my doctor or lawyer told me to do something, I did it. I am paying someone else to give me a recommendation and I should take it. Approach your sales approach in the same way. You are the one being paid to make a recommendation; you are the expert they are looking for to help out with their decision.

When a customer calls me and wants to know what I feel would be the best leasing option for their situation I gather the information I need and then make a recommendation based off of that information. I assume the authority figure status. Elvis was that professional. You knew whatever he was going to sing it would be a great presentation to what he felt and believed. You are paying for the presentation, take it and use the information to your advantage.

Don't give your best deal on the front end; you will have no place to go. This is a mistake new sales people make all the time. Again go back to Elvis. He was not going to come out and sing "American Trilogy" as his first song. Where would he go from there? You have to leave yourself an out. Part of my responsibility of working for the music store was that every other Saturday I would be required to work a shift in the store. As much as I did not want to work in the store or especially on a Saturday it was a great learning time since I would be around my peers who sold on a daily basis. I learned there are new habits to new sales people. As a rule we had the authority to give up to a 20% discount across the board without any permission from upper management. This was one of the most abused authorities I ever saw.

We had a new young sales person working in the store. He was a high school student who had no experience in a sales environment. One of his first sales was a guitar with a sticker price of around $1000. He knew he could go up to 20% off and so anxious to close the sale he made an offer to the customer that still to this day makes me think before I act. He offered a 20% discount on the guitar if the customer would also purchase a case to go along with it. The case had a retail of around $125. The customer of course took the offer. Think about this now, what my young sales person friend had done was give the case away and still discounted the guitar. He would have been better off to reduce the price of the guitar by 5% and still give the case away. He could have netted another $25 on the sale. It is important to see what is best for you and the customer. The presentation of a free case could have closed the sale without any discount. This is a common mistake among new sales people. I have made the same mistake myself. Don't give away the farm just to make a sale. You also have to make a profit in order for you to get a commission. Don't get me wrong there are times when you need to take a loss in order to get something else down the line. Sometimes it is good business to just make the sale.

In the example above, the sales person did everything right accept the price. He had the right presentation. He was knowledgeable about the product. He made himself out to be the authority figure. He even went as far as to make an offer for acceptance. He just made the incorrect offer. Be careful about what you offer. Make sure it makes good sense for the customer and the company. I feel like the customer will come back to purchase again from this person not because he thought he was a good sales person but because he thinks he may be able to get something for nothing. This portrays the wrong impression and the wrong way to create loyalty from the customer. He won the battle but lost the war so to speak.

Make yourself the authority figure and make the sale. Make sure it is good for both parties. You do not have to make all your money on one transaction. Remember the way Elvis sold---it is all about the presentation. If you are well prepared and present well you will make the sale.

Selling is a piece of C.A.K.E.

Ok, you have wanted to know how easy C.A.K.E. is since the first time I mentioned it. C.A.K.E. will allow you to become and understand the sales habits of the most successful sales people in the industry. If you use

C.A.K.E. to your advantage and apply it to every sales presentation, not just some of them, you will become great.

> Confidence
> Attitude
> Knowledge
> Execution

My past supervisor taught this to me some years ago as the basis to all selling. It is a great tool to help understand the presentation and how to relate this concept to any sales opportunity. Michael Hall's presentation and philosophy is this: They are not in the correct order; the order should actually be Attitude, Knowledge, Confidence and then Execution. You have to have the attitude to gain the knowledge to get the confidence to be able to execute. I know of several people that have the knowledge but no confidence or they have the wrong attitude and cannot execute effectively. The C.A.K.E. concept will only work if you employ all of it. Utilize all the components to be able to achieve the correct goal of execution. To execute does not just mean to make a presentation but to do it effectively. In order to be effective you will need to first obtain the attitude to gain the knowledge to have the confidence to make the execution. It is as easy as C.A.K.E.

Confidence is the first and foremost component to the sales tool. You must be confident but not arrogant. You have heard of the term a "con-man or confidence man". The concept is to convey your confidence to others. I am not telling you to "con" people but to act with confidence and help others to see your confidence and understand it. Back to Elvis, Elvis was one of the most confident people I have seen. He was borderline arrogant and sometimes all the way over the line. This is sometimes a trait among us sales people. Michael Hall demonstrates this in a strong and good way in everything he does he is confident without being arrogant. In the way he walks and in his demeanor as well as his selling style. If you are timid and can't portray this level of confidence you can get in trouble in a sales call very quickly. I assure you that you have never been to a doctor who was not confident about telling you to stick out your tongue. He knew what he needed you to do to progress with the call and he let you know this. When Michael gets on a call he knows what he wants the outcome to be and is confident about his presentation and quickly becomes the authority figure even in situations he may not be the most knowledgeable about. He convinces you to see his confidence in yourself. I always leave Michael feeling good about myself. This is a hard lesson to teach people who have spent their entire career trying to master this trait. Michael does it with the best of them.

Have you ever been to a flea market or garage sale and had a non-confident person try to sell you something? They usually start out with a negative question something like "you don't want this swing to go with that wagon?" No I don't. No confidence from this person. You can tell they are afraid to make the sale. If they do it is by pure luck. I have even had sales people go as far as shake their head no when making a statement like this. I remember a trip to Mexico when a street vendor stated to me "you don't want this necklace?" this situation could be completely changed with a little confidence. Example: "This swing would go great with that wagon" or tell them you are confident with a phrase like "I am confident that your wife will love the necklace" or "The best computer you could purchase for your application would be the one with the 1 gig processor" you can never go wrong with a strong confident statement.

Attitude is the next issue. What type of attitude do you come across with? Is your attitude one of "you need my help" or "let me help you"?

I have had sales people come to my door selling everything from cookies to newspapers to wanting to mow my yard. One instance of attitude came in the fashion of a sales person who could not understand when no was no and when no was a smokescreen. He was selling magazine subscriptions. When I answered the door, he greeted me correctly and told me what he was doing and for what cause. I listened to his presentation and then refused his offer. His attitude was to continue as if I had said nothing. At first I found this amusing and also smart. He blew right past my rejection. Good start but he went a bit too far. After his second attempt to close me on the sale I again refused only this time a bit more forcefully and made it clear I was not interested. He responded with a question "why?" This was the last straw. I was not going to buy anything from this kid no matter what it was and even if I needed it. If he was selling water in the desert I was not buying. His attitude was wrong. That was it, nothing else. His presentation and confidence was good but wrong attitude. He lost the sale although he had all the correct tools.

This taught me a good lesson. You have to be strong and confident and sometimes even a little pushy. It is not a bad thing to put forth a strong attitude just make sure you understand the attitude you are showing your customers. Back to the attitude of the doctor or the lawyer, they have the attitude that if they make a recommendation to do something you will. When a customer comes into your store or to your car lot they are coming for advice on which item to purchase. Do you have the confidence and the right attitude to help them?

A good tool to use is to record or videotape yourself. In school I was in an education class where we had to get up and teach a lesson to the rest of the class as an assignment. I learned more about my own confidence and attitude by watching that tape than anyone could have taught me or told me. To this day I still record myself giving my presentation to check to make sure I am following my own advice. Make sure you have the correct attitude. Ask others to help you with this one.

Knowledge: are you knowledgeable about your subject and your product? Do you actually know what you are selling or what business you are in? The President of the Rolex watch company was once asked at a business lunch how the watch business was going. He replied "I have no idea how the watch business is. I am not in the watch business". To the surprise of the person asking, he stated "You are the President of the most famous watch company in the world and you don't know how the watch business is going?" To this the President replied "I am not in the watch business, I am in the luxury business and the luxury business is doing great!" This might sound funny to you but the point here is to really deeply understand what your business is. Are you in the car business or the luxury car business, the leasing business or the financial solutions business, the office supplies business or the time saving business? Take time to study what it is you do and how it affects other people.

Do you know everything about your products and business? I am in the leasing industry. I have been leasing or financing products since starting at the music store over 11 years ago. Am I in the sales field, the leasing field, or the financial solutions field? Most of the time, I wear several different hats. I am actually in all 3 fields. Sometimes the only subject to a sales call is leasing when other times I am speaking with someone who knows nothing about leasing but knows everything about the product. At this point, I am in the sales business and need to be able to apply sales techniques to my presentation rather than leasing strategies. In the same conversation, the topic can very quickly change to benefits of leasing over purchasing out right. At this point I have now become the financial solutions provider. In all of these subjects I maintain myself as the authority figure and make sure I am knowledgeable about whichever subject we are on.

I know people in my industry that know the end and outs to the product they sell much better than anyone out there. They can tell you how to and actually build a computer from scratch. But they fail on a daily basis because they don't understand what it is they actually do. They are knowledgeable about their product but not there service. You have to be able to not only understand your products but also be able to show what benefits they have to others when you are making a presentation. Remember it is not what you say but how you say it.

You may have gone to your local automotive store or electronics store or even the office supplies store to look for an item you may not know anything about. Your sales person is what we call in the sales field as a "techie" or someone who is very technical in their speech and presentation of the item they have to show you. I don't know about you but I get lost very quickly. They talk over my head so to speak. The sales person has all the knowledge in the world but is actually failing in the sales process because they have turned me off on the sale. My wife and I have a new child and went to the Mall to look at video recorders. The first place I went was a camera shop. The sales person started talking about pixel and clarification and terms I was not familiar with. In a matter of minutes I was not hearing a thing he said. He was one of the most knowledgeable sales people I had met about the products he had to offer but failed to close the sale due to his presentation.

Knowledge is a valuable and dangerous tool when used correctly can save the sale but when used wrong can prevent you from making the current sale or any future sales. The customer does not want to come back to you because they don't want a lecture on what they want or what you have to show them. Again, it is all about presentation and make sure you understand your place in the sales process. You are not the only one in the process but merely a guide or advisor on how to achieve a mutual goal between sales and what the customer needs and wants.

Execution of your plan is the last and item in C.A.K.E. To execute is to complete the transaction. When is the sale complete? When you finish the presentation or when you have given all the benefits? No, the sale is over and executed when the customer purchases the product you are offering to them. Don't ever forget or confuse effort or work with results. I have always made the statement to measure performance and execution by results. Some of the best presenters are the worst executors. Why? Did you know that in a national survey somewhere between 65% and 69% of all sales calls end without the sales person asking for the order? The sales person failed to execute his plan. Have a plan of execution and execute your plan.

When I started with Dell Financial Services I sat across from a girl who had 0 sales experience. She would take the same amount of calls as I did and somehow never managed to close as many deals or make quota. I started listening to her to find out what we were doing different from each other. It was simple and after bringing it to her attention her close rate almost doubled. She was not asking for the order.

At the end of your presentation all of that effort is lost if you cannot execute and close the sale. In a face to face meeting I have found it best if at the end of your presentation you push yourself back from the table and make a statement "Now this is what I would like to do" and proceed to tell the customer what you would like to do. Follow up with "Can I write the order up for you", "How would you like to pay for this new car", "Are you going to be setting this account up as a joint or individual account?" What are you doing in all these instances? You are asking for the order. There is only one way to mess the execution part of the sale up and that is not to ask. Do you want to be one of the 60 some odd percent that does not ever ask for the order?

The girl next to me started using one catch phrase and ultimately started making quota and performing up to her standard. Her secret close was simple. The same one I used to obtain the highest close rate on the leasing floor. "Mr. Customer, is there any reason why you cannot send back the lease documents today?" That is it, it is this simple. It is not always how you ask but just the fact that you ask.

I have also heard poor presentations that ended up with a sale because the sales person got at least the execution part of the system down. They asked for the sale and got it.

One of the fun things I like to do after I ask for the sale is to just be quiet and listen. The next person to speak is the one being sold. If the customer states that they can send the docs back right away than you have done your job. If the customer states that they need to speak with their spouse then you know that the deal is not closed and you need to go back and revisit the question. However, if you pipe in and try to close again before the customer states the answer, you are losing the sale and the customer has just taken away your confidence, your attitude, your knowledge and your execution. Again, someone is going to get sold is it you or the customer?

Summary

I could stop right here. If you follow these suggestions you will succeed at being one of the best sales people around. We will go into more specific applications in later chapters. Remember a few simple things:

Quality not always quantity

Believe in your product and believe in yourself. It is very difficult to show the positive side to a product and make your case if you don't believe in it yourself.

Do business with top people. Make sure the one you are making your presentation to is the one who can make the decision.

Anthony Robbins states that "Success should be studied and is not a mistake". Study top producers around you to find out what they are doing and why they are on top. I see a lot of new sales people that try to do just the opposite and stay away from the top producers. Not me, I want to know how they got to the top and try to imitate what they do. The first day at my current job the first thing I did was look at the daily sales report to see who was at the top of their game. After finding out who was the top producer I made my request to sit with this person and be trained by them. It was not but about a month or so before that person moved up in the company and I took their place as one of the top producers in my division. People want to buy from top producers within their field. If you go to buy a house do you want to deal with the top sales person or the new guy who is the worst one in the sales force? I don't know about you, but I will take the number one guy every time. Top producers plan and organize.

Make sure you are the authority figure. 71% of all sales are made on "trust" as the prime factor in the sale.

If you remember nothing else about chapter one, remember C.A.K.E. and always ask for the sale!

Chapter 2
Why and what people buy

1. Why people buy?
   a. Emotions
   b. China eggs
   c. Loyalty
   d. F.U.D.
2. What people buy?

Do you really understand why and what people buy? Zig Zigler's comment is not to be a "wandering generality". In other words, don't be a person that just wanders around doing general things. Understand why and what you do. Make sure you understand the buying trends of your customers. Sales are not a game of throwing something up on the wall and seeing what sticks. I know several sales people that do operate this way and do okay in their field. They are not top producers but most of the time they have a general understanding of what they do. I know you have heard the expression that you cannot hit a goal you do not have or cannot see. Don't wander around trying to hit goals that you can't see. Understand why and what people buy. Top producers are a student of the game. They do the common things uncommonly well!

Why people buy?

People generally buy on **emotion**. People act more quickly out of fear of loss than a desire for gain. This is pure emotion kicking in. We will discuss the fear factor later in the chapter. Remember me stating that people will buy from you because they like you? I also stated that a sale is 85% emotion. People want to feel rather than think. When you go to purchase a new car, how do you pick it out? You pick the one you want by the way it looks or feels to you. Not what the salesman thinks of it. This is a very important lesson to understand early in a sales person's career if you can keep in check with your emotions and the customer's emotions, you can make it happen.

When making a sales call take into account the customers emotions and how you make your presentation. On large ticket items people are looking at the emotional effect a monthly payment will make on them. When I was on the road and leasing a musical instrument to a new band student's parents, I always sold the monthly payment and not the amount of the instrument. People will consider the purchase more if you can sell the monthly payment. I personally don't want to purchase a $30,000 dollar automobile but I will purchase a $400 dollar a month automobile because the $400 dollars relates to my emotions that I can afford a monthly payment of $400 dollars a month but I cannot afford a $30,000 dollar car. Which feels better to you a $1200 dollar saxophone or a monthly lease payment of $89 bucks? I have made several sales where the customer never knew what the actual retail price of an item was but they knew they could afford the monthly payment. I have also found if you will phrase your questions correctly you will have better results. After the presentation, ask the customer how it feels to them rather than what they think. Again people don't want to think about the decision they want to feel like they made the right choice. You will get two completely different answers when you ask how do feel rather than what do you think. When you ask what do you think you will almost always get the answer "I think we need to discuss it more" or "I think the rate is two high", but when you ask how do you feel about this you will get responses like "I feel like this will work" or "I really like this color". The concept of selling off a person's emotion is not a new one but it is often not used correctly.

Another way I like to use the emotion factor is to ask the question "Do you feel this will meet your need?" You want to ask open-ended questions and this is a good one. They will either say yes it does or tell you why it doesn't. Then you can start to overcome the objections to close the sale. The emotion factor can come into play almost every time. Even if the customer is ready to purchase they sometimes have their emotions working on how they will pay or what color they want. The use of emotions in selling dates back to biblical times when chariots and swords were leased for battle. They made the swords shiny and decorated them with jewels even though this made no practical application to the usefulness of the weapon. They already understood that emotions came into play if you wanted to sell or lease your products you had to relate to the senses of the buyer.

On larger ticket items leasing or financing is a great selling tool. If you have in-house leasing or a finance structure you will find that the average sale that is leased is about 15% higher than a sale that is a cash transaction. Again consumers will pay another $10 a month to get leather seats in their new car, but they do not want to spend $1000 cash. The best advice you can give to your customers is purchase what appreciates and lease what depreciates. Use your capitol to make more money don't spend your cash on an asset that depreciates like a car or computer. There are also certain advantages to cash flow and total cost of ownership in leasing. You will come out better in a cash flow situation if you pay $300 a month over 3 years than to put out $8000 at one time and try to recoup the capitol over the same period of time.

In addition to emotion, people will also buy out of need and want. Several customers have already decided to buy but this is something you will need to find out for yourself. Customers will not always buy and sometimes you lose the sale. This was probably the hardest lesson for me to learn about when a customer was ready to purchase. Make sure the customer buys from you. This goes back directly to what Guy was always trying to tell me "never say buy and never say sell". You have to deal with the customer's emotions in order to fully understand the sales process.

"Don't sit on China Eggs"

What is a China Egg? A China egg is an egg that no matter how long you sit on it, it is not going to hatch. In the car business the phrase is a "tire kicker". Be careful how you use your time with "tire kickers" and "china eggs". It is real easy to sit on these types of deal and put hour after hour into trying to close the sale and the customer has no intention to purchase. They may be using you for information or just have not made up their mind as well as may not be able to afford your product. In my brief extent at selling insurance I ran into a "china egg" that I sat on and sat on knowing it was going to hatch. I spoke with the customer over and over again. He never had a problem telling me yes but he could not come through with the money. Remember again that the sale is complete when the customer purchases from you. (A sale is not measured by the amount of time put into the transaction.) I have spent days and days closing a $5000 dollar leasing transaction and only fifteen minutes closing a $100,000 dollar transaction. Again, I have also sat on a few china eggs.

As I stated earlier sometimes no matter what you do or how you do it you will lose the sale. I hate to loose. When I can't close the sale I feel like it is my fault and sometimes it really bothers me. I have to remind myself all the time that this is not the case. Sometimes the customer is just not ready. They may be ready later down the line or never at all. I know that all of us have thought about a purchase that we did not go through with. Maybe it was a jet ski or boat, a pool or hot tub or even something as small as a pet or fish tank. You went to the store to gather information and to decide if you could afford it. Someone at the store helped you and in there mind had a big sale going. You decided not to purchase at this time, maybe after even several trips to the same store and with the same salesperson. The time was just not right. The first lesson for the salesperson is that he or she will make that sale. It may be tomorrow or the next day but the sale will come.

My first boss at the music store, Gil, taught me this lesson within the first week I was there. There is no difference between retail and real estate, insurance and instruments. Sometimes the sale is not going to happen with this customer. Rest assured that the sale will happen. You will sell that car or hot tub. I was in the music store on a Saturday and I think it may have been my first week to work there. Eager to make a sale, I was referred to a customer looking for a drum set. As I was a drummer and knew the product I was chosen to help the customer. I went over every feature I knew. I think I even made up a few. I used every closing tool at once. I offered the customer a free stick bag, stool, and discounted the system. I did everything but offer to go home with them and help set it up. The customer walked and I lost the sale. This is when Gil pulled me aside and taught me a valuable lesson. You will make the sale; don't worry about it he told me. We are in retail and there will be several more times in the next few days that someone will come in looking for a drum set.

The very next day I made the sale and was actually able to do it on a better deal for the company. I made several hundred more dollars in commission on the sale than I would have if I sold the set the day before. This was a good lesson learned and a good one to remember. I could have sat on that "china egg" and never made the sale no matter how much effort I put forth. The second thing I have somewhere on my desk, usually next to the Elvis picture is a 5X7 card that states in big red letters "don't sit on china eggs".

Another reason people will do business with you is out of **loyalty**. A few things to remember, I made a statement earlier that 71% of all sales are made on "trust" as the prime factor. Loyalty builds this trust. To this day I pick a gas station to trade with and try to go to it every time even if one day it is higher than another. I know in the long run I will come out ahead. Be loyal to your customer and expect them to be loyal with you. You must build a relationship with your customers. I always tried to call on one customer a day at lunchtime. I have done as much business over lunch as in the whole day. Deals are made and lost over a meal. You buy the meal whether the customer purchases today or not. You are building and demanding loyalty from your customers.

After saying this, there is a fine line between a relationship and going to far. In the same respect you never want to date or just hang out with customers that could influence the way they look at you from an authority figure. If a customer becomes mad or upset at your personality, I assure you they will not do as much business. You may not lose the account but it will never be the same again.

If you are in the insurance business or deal with business owners a lot, try breakfast. I had a friend of mine who made all his calls at breakfast. He would sometimes schedule more than one a day. Just eat light at both meals. Guess what? He is at the top of his sales force. People were loyal to him and are more open to suggestions when they are fresh in the morning and also when they are not hungry.

Make sure that you go by this rule in your every day life as well in how you deal with loyalty towards people. I go to the same gas station every day; I know in the long run you will come out better. I also use the same dry cleaners and go to the same grocery store and try to deal with the same clerk at the bank. It is very important that you demand loyalty but also that you are loyal.

Other ways to help build loyalty is through taking care of the customers needs even if they are not what you think their needs are. I have had several customers become friends and confide in me about their working environment or home life. One year at Thanksgiving I even had one of my customers come over for dinner because he was going to be by himself. Needless to say this customer became one of the most loyal customers. If your customer is selling cookies for their kid or candles for their wives buy from them without hesitation. In the music business I would always purchase raffle tickets or candy from the band members. If the money was going to help out the school or the overall account I was in on it. Be loyal to your customers and they will be loyal to you. If one of my customers was ever considering purchasing from another vendor, most of the time they would tell me about it. Or they would ask for advice on what or whom to consider in their effort to maximize their budgets. Losing a small sale every once in a while would ultimately land me the big deals that I worked so hard for.

Customer gifts are a subject that you need to be careful with. Never give monetary gifts. Use gifts wisely. Send gifts that will last a while or not be easily forgotten. Every Christmas I used to send out subscriptions of Readers Digest to of all my clients that I had worked with over the entire year. Why Readers Digest? Well I knew that it would not be controversial or contents questionable. I also knew that it would come to the customer each and every month during the year. This reminds the customer once a month when they receive the magazine of who sent it to them. Me. Even if I was not going to see them for a week or so they still would remember who gave them the gift and that I would be coming to see them soon. This became a very successful tool for my overall performance. Use common sense, I know of several very successful salespeople that never send gifts. This is fine too if you can find other ways to make the customer think of you other than the bill they receive on the first of every month. End result is always the same, build the relationship to one of loyalty and make sure the customer thinks of you or your product even when you are not around.

F.U.D.

F.U.D. is a sales tool implemented from IBM, Inc I think back in the sixties. It is a fundamental sales tool that is still a great basic concept to any presentation. F.U.D. is another way to help with the overall picture of the presentation. Fear, Uncertainty and Doubt is the basic fundamental. If you can bestow one of these core fundamental conditions in the mind of the customer you will always have a better chance to close the sale. People act more quickly out of the fear of loss rather than a desire for gain. Think about the old car salesman who would make the statement "If you want this car we need to go ahead and get it now because I have two other people coming to look at in the morning" What it this salesperson trying to do? Although crude he is trying to bestow a sense of fear that you may lose the car if you don't act immediately. This is really not what I mean with fear of loss. You can create a sense of fear without being crude.

You can be honest and still get the F.U.D. factor going to help close the sale. In the leasing and finance field, specials and rates change sometimes daily. Be honest, sales are not about cheating people but about helping them meet their needs, wants and desires. F.U.D. is why you see marketing information like "for a limited time" or "offer ends tomorrow" or my favorite "not available in stores". Ron Popeal and his Ronco Inc. do F.U.D. with the best of them. I was watching an infomercial over the weekend with Ron doing the presentation. He used various terms like the ones above along with a pricing scheme to make any presentation a success. Ron stated "The price of this item is not $300 dollars or even $200 dollars but 3 easy payments of $39.95". This statement was met with cheers from the audience.

"Only three easy payments of $39.95" This statement sums up presentation. He sells the monthly payment without ever giving the total price of the item followed up by a statement of "This is a special TV offer not available in stores". This creates a since of fear, uncertainty and doubt that if you don't purchase now you will not be able to later, and this price is only for the TV viewers. This is a great example of F.U.D.

The other F.U.D. statement that is also a closing statement is "If you call in the next 15 minutes we will include at no charge this great set of steak knives". Any way that you can create a sense of urgency you will win more often than not. You can use a closing tool to help create the F.U.D. factor and you should.

Ever wonder why prices are stated like they are? $19.95 instead of $20 dollars? It even looks better. It is a simple way to play on your emotions. You don't want to spend $20 but $19.95 looks too much like only $19 so this is why prices are stated just below the item. In ads that come from the grocery store they are always dated with an expiration date to encourage a sense of urgency.

The Fear you will lose the item along with the uncertainty that the price will stay the same and last the doubt that you will never get this chance again to purchase the item of your dreams. This is a great sales tool that can make the difference between you making the sale and the customer creating the same sense of F.U.D in you the sales person. Remember you are the professional.

What people buy?

As important as it is to understand why people buy you must also have a good idea what people buy. You are probably saying to yourself well people will buy almost anything. This is true but not really what I am referring to. People generally will purchase based on four things: manufacturer, product, service or price in almost this order. Notice that price is the last reason people will purchase an item.

We would all purchase a Mercedes based on manufacturer, product and service. Price is what came into play on this one. But I feel like price is not really the concern. If you could find a way to get the monthly payment to under $450 a month then you would have a new Mercedes sitting in your driveway tonight. When I say price I am really referring to the whole picture and not just the full retail figure.

Manufacturer is the first on the list. People every year spend millions of dollars on Ralph Lauren clothes just because the brand is Ralph Lauren. This is a good example of how people will purchase an item because of the manufacturer. I could make a list of several manufacturers that have just as good of quality clothes but they do not have the little polo horse on the pocket. The price is usually not the issue.

I keep making a big deal about price because most of us think that price is the major reason why people will purchase. Price does fit into the solution but it is far from the primary reason. Although most customers will try to tell you that it is. I know of several times when I was looking to purchase an item for myself, I had already made up my mind that I would purchase but asked for a better price just to see if I could get it. Don't make price the main point in you presentation.

The product is the second thing people look to when ready to purchase. What product do customers look for? Think about this for a minute, if a customer is looking for a typewriter, they are not going to buy anything but a typewriter. They may not have decided to buy it from you but the product is already decided on. I cannot tell you of one instance where a customer came into one of my stores to purchase beer and I sold them water. Not one time did a customer come into the music store to look at drums and I sold them a banjo. The product is decided on and the customer, if serious, will stick to this product.

Service is what I feel like to be one of the most important factors and will in a lot of instances overcome the price. At Dell Computer Corporation, they pride themselves on their award winning service. Whether it is tech support or the customer service department, they feel that service will make the sale when nothing else will.

Back to the car dealers who may not have the best price but will give me an additional one year service warranty. Service comes at a price.

While traveling on the road servicing the school music programs across Texas, I often sold my products on the point of service. I had the conversation often that sure you could order the product from a mail order catalog and save maybe 10% on the front end but who is standing in your office? Is the mail order company going to be there when you need to service that item or if it comes in damaged? This also goes back to loyalty along with service. If you are loyal to your customers and give them great service you will get repeat business. There were even times when service came into favors or out of the way service items. I would often pick up a large item from one school that was going to borrow it from another. No charge for helping out I was going that way anyway and this creates a service level that is unprecedented in today's sales field. I would also bring up several other points to price. The most important to me was when I would get in a price discussion, my response of "On top of every other benefit, you also get me and I will not only deliver the item to your door but I will also take you out to lunch when I do it." The next thing I would always remind the customer about loyalty was I was going to be there every week throughout the year. That in itself is a service and service comes at a price to have the very best.

Sometimes you can even sell the service for a price. Most companies will have a maintenance or service agreement that can be purchased in addition to the price of the item. These items are very easy most of the time to include with the product and add to the bottom line in commissions for each sale. People want service on there products. I have won a lot of sales even when the price was higher because of the service factor. At the music store, we had a simple maintenance agreement that was only $3.00 a month on top of the monthly payment. I never sold an instrument without having this service attached to the agreement. It was and still is a great sales tool not only to help the customer overcome a need for service but also a great way for you to increase you total overall production by 2 or 3 percent.

Price is the last item that will cause a person to purchase. I put it at the last because if everything else is in place manufacturer, product and service you can win most of the time over price. I am not always the lowest price in leasing but our service and ease of contract is so good it overcomes the price objection. You will have to learn through your own experience how to overcome the price concern. You will have to address it and sometimes but very rarely lose because of it. Most of the time you lose because of price or what the customer tells you, price was actually not the issue at all. Customers understand that there is a price associated with an item and that you do get what you pay for. That is why discount stores don't sell Dell Computers or Ralph Lauren shirts.

Sometimes price is the only condition and this is why I include it on the list. If you find someone only interested in price they are most likely a bargain hunter. Price is the only thing they will look at and no matter what you do the service and product will not come into play. This is why pawnshops have great success. The customer that frequents a pawnshop usually is looking for one thing, price. Be price conscience and know where and how low you can go to win the deal. Just make the sale. You can use price to your advantage if you have a finance program and can sometimes make a larger sale on the front end because your rates beat out the competition. I can always sell a larger ticket item if I can make the monthly payment come out to what the customer wants it to be. You can stretch the payment out on a 48-month term rather than a 36-month to get the payment lower than the competition. Even though the customer pays more in the long run you can sometimes win the price war with the finance option.

Remember after you have convinced the customer to buy from you they have to have a way to pay for the product. You will have to establish a funding source for the products that the customer is looking for and give discounts accordingly. You can use a cash buy as one to beat price and offer the largest discount if the customer will pay in full. Use price to your advantage and get creative with how much and when to get into a price war.

The customer has four things they are looking for manufacturer, product, service and price. You do not have to win over all these points to get the sale usually if you have two of the four you will be in good shape. If you will remember this when you go to work for a company and work for one that has a strong product and reputation for service you will be halfway there.

Chapter 3
Preparing for the Sale

1. Presentation
   a. 10-3-1
   b. Skills
2. Breakdown of the sales call
3. Difference between types of calls
   a. Face to Face
   b. Phone
4. Secret to closing the sale

   a. Overcoming objections
   b. Referrals
   c. Closing tools

As I have said several times, the **presentation** is everything. If you can perfect this aspect of selling you are on your way to a successful career. You must prepare for the sale as you would for any other event in your life. You don't want to go into a situation blind or not understanding where you are in the process. The first thing I would do is to try to understand what type of sales person you are. There are basically four types of sales people closers, techies, charismatics and passives.

Which one is best? I believe that a good mix of all four is the best. Let's look at each one to try to understand how they each will relate to you.

The first is the closer. The closer is the one that is asking for the sale from the very start. They will usually try to position the sale early and may ask for the sale several times throughout the process. Just a note: the closers will have of course the highest close rate but also the highest return and lowest customer satisfaction rate. The next is the techie. The techie is the knowledgeable one that always talks over your head. They will know more about the product than the manufacturer and wants to show you what they know. Sometimes the techie will intimidate you into the sale because of the customer's own lack of knowledge about the product. The third is the charismatic or I like to call the used car salesman persona. This is the person that is overly cheerful and agrees with everything you say. Charismatics are usually top sales people by sheer numbers because they will talk to anyone and everyone. Sometimes they come across as being phony. Passives are the type that will always be your friends. They will usually build strong relationships but not always top performers. Try to understand your selling type and use it to your advantage to help you make the sale. I will go into the customer types and "color" types in Chapter 4 which will also help to better understand what and why you sell the way you do. It is equally important to understand your own selling style, as it is to understand the customer and how to make the correct presentation. Again, I believe that the best selling style is the one that can combine all these and use each one as it is needed in the presentation.

10-3-1 Rule

The 10-3-1 rule generally applies to cold or prospecting calls. What this means is simple: it takes 10 calls to get 3 people to let you give your pitch to get 1 person to purchase. Unless you are lucky enough to be in a captive type of sales position or an after the sales type of service person this rule will generally hold true. This rule will apply to most sales that are deemed not immediate purchases such as insurance, cars, or sometimes homes. With this in mind what we can determine is that the more calls you do the more sales you will make. Simple!! However most good sales people have never heard this before or tried to apply it to their everyday routine. The first step is to determine how many sales you need to make in a given period of time. If you need to make 5 sales a day then by the shear number of the rule you would need to make 50 calls to get 12 people to actually let you make a presentation to get 5 to purchase. Don't go home for the day until you have made the 50 calls. If you make the 12 presentations you are on the right track. Even if all 5 don't purchase right away the number will all fall into place. It is the law of averages that is in your favor. Selling is a science and can be calculated in several different ways. There is no need to re-invent the wheel. This is one of the most successful tools in the car business. If you need to sell 5 cars a day then try to talk to at least 50 people a day. If you are cold calling for an appointment such in the case of a stockbroker or insurance sales you will find that this math almost always holds true. You will need to make 50 cold calls to find 12 people that are interested enough in your product in order to make 5 sales. If you follow this simple math you will come out ahead. After you have successfully made all your calls for the day and are walking out the office, challenge yourself to go back to your desk and make just one more call. You will be amazed how this will add up to the bottom line on your total performance and your success overall not to mention your close rate and also improve on the 10-3-1 rule of sale. I always like to refer back to Babe Ruth. At the time Babe Ruth held the record for the most home run hits. He also held the record for the most strikeouts in one year. The Babe actually was using the 10-3-1 rule in his baseball career. He swung at everything knowing that the more times he swung at the ball the more chance of hitting a home run became possible. Also remember that such greats like Nolan Ryan, who in his first season as a pro, had the worst record in the league and walked more than any other pitcher that year. As you know Ryan went on to hold the record for the most strikeouts. Sometimes you will have to go through a lot of sales calls before scoring big but if you stick with it and utilize the 10-3-1 concept you too will hold a top sales record in your sales career.

Skills

There are several sales skills that you need to be aware of before you make a presentation. The first I can tell you is to know your own product backwards and forwards not only the hardware but also the software. What I mean by this is don't only know everything there is to know about the actual item such as the car or computer but also know the contract you expect the customer to sign. In other words read your own contract. I cannot stress how important it is to know what you are asking a customer to sign. At Caldwell Music I would present the same contract to lease a musical instrument sometimes as many as fifty times over a four or five hour period. You need to be on your toes and be able to answer simple questions about what your contract says. The first recommendation to you right now is to put this book down and get your hands on a copy of your own contract. Pick it apart, try to find the loopholes you would want and the questions you would have if you were signing the agreement yourself. The other contract you need to know about is your competitions. Find out what they are doing and what they expect out of their customers. If you know how your competitions' contract works this will allow you to point out the strong points in your own contract. Along with this make sure that you also know your competition as well. I regularly make a call and pretend to be a customer interested in what my competitor is selling. I also make calls to my own company and to my own customer service to better understand the customer's point of view.

Make sure that you know the situation you are going into. If on a sales call or appointment calls make sure you try to find out anything and everything you can about the company or individual. Visit your customer's website and read about their products or ideas. If you are going to need to present numbers or suggestions make sure you are well prepared in advance. Take samples with you in order to look and feel more professional along with creating the correct presentation. Have responses for objections. Know what the top 10 or 20 objections are for a particular product. You will also need to practice overcoming these same objections. Make sure you are ready when the question or the word "no" comes up. If you are doing phone sales you can create a sample or cheat sheet with the top objections and keep it handy in case it comes up. And it will come up.

Practice different ways to "trial close". Understand when is the correct time to stop making your presentation and when it is time to write the contract that you have already read and know almost word for word. Just be well prepared for the call and don't ever enter into a situation you are not comfortable with. Practice these skills.

Make sure that you know your own work habits. Do you know what your strengths and weaknesses are? Do you know what time of the day, week, or month are your best chances and your best time to close sales? (Do you know your own close rate not only overall but when you close rate is at its highest?) Do you know when you are the happiest and when you are at you saddest or lowest time at your job or in your day? All these questions need to be answered. I know you have heard the phrase "You cannot manage what you cannot measure". You need to make sure you are your own manager first.

Statistically showing is that somewhere around 75% of business is done between 10:00 a.m. and 3:00 p.m. Are you working the hardest during these times? Also, you are more likely to reach people for an appointment between 8:00 a.m. and 10:00 a.m. Always try to schedule your outbound times during this span since you should be fresh and ready to go. Remember from a previous chapter that you should be coming back from your first appointment of the day around 8:00 am. This should have been your breakfast appointment and now you will need to come down after that first sale you just made before even going to the office. Think of how good it will feel to go into the office at 8:00 am and telling your co-workers that you have already closed a sale over breakfast.

One of the most valuable skills that should always be at the top of the list is your Positive Mental Attitude. This is why I made it the last skill on the list. Please remember that you only get one chance to make a first impression. Keep your head about you. Be positive and confident. Remember to be on your best behavior. I have seen a lot of great deals go south because of the pure attitude of the salesperson. Remember to be excited about what you are doing and what you are selling. Have you ever been speaking with a salesperson that would tell you not to buy their product? I have. I have actually had a salesperson tell me "Oh, you don't want this item. It is not made well and you would be better to look at another store". Needless to say, the next time I went into the same store the salesperson was no longer with the company.

Breakdown of the sales call

Let's get into the actual meat of the sales call. I am going to approach this as if you are making a person-to-person presentation. I will go more in depth as to different situations in the next sub chapter pertaining to areas of differences between phone presentations and cold calls. Let's approach as a warm or repeat customer and face-to-face.

First of all, be prepared and have a plan. Make sure that your shoes are polished and your clothes are neat and pressed. Get a hair cut every 2 weeks whether you need it or not. Did you check your breath? If you are using visual aids and an agenda (which you should be) make sure they are also clean and neat. Take this opportunity to make the first impression a good one.

Follow these simple steps and you will be on your way to becoming great!

The first thing you will encounter is the greeting. This is your chance for small talk and to find out how much time the customer has to spend with you. One of the first things I always do is establish a time frame as to how long I have to make the presentation. "Mr. Customer, how much time do we have this afternoon that we can discuss how I can help?" After this question, wait for the customer to let you know how much time you have. The next main thing is to stick to this time frame. You will always get the next appointment if you can follow this time frame rule. Reiterate your time frame and make your presentation of an agenda for the customers review. Yes, ask the customer to review the agenda that you have prepared and ask for there approval to make sure you are discussing the proper ideas of the customer.

Face to Face

First of all keep your agenda short, only four or five items, and always leave an open spot for the customer to discuss their questions or opinions. Make your agenda a one-page item in large bold type and make it look very clean. When the customer tells you how much time they have write it down on the top of your agenda page and make sure the customer sees it. After you present the customer with your agenda ask for their approval to continue. Below is a sample:

Today's date
Leave a line for time allotted

1. Why you are here and about my company

2. Discuss your needs, wants and desires

3. Recommendations for your company's solutions

4. Open (your questions or opinions)

5. Recommendations from the customer

6. Finalizations

This is a very simple and good agenda to use and can be customized to any situation. If you have the luxury of being able to take a laptop computer with you on sales calls have this in a word format that you can change with the customer looking at it. Again make sure you make notes in the open spot as the customer tells you what they need and get your customers approval for what you are discussing today.

Let's look at the breakdown. The first on the list is "Why you are here and about my company". This is the spot to create the expectation of what your goal is and what you can do for the customer. Explain why you want to talk to them and give the strengths of your company. Use simple terms to describe your company like we are manufacture connected or the second largest. Maybe you have recently been able to help with another customer in the same field. Tell your strengths.

The second topic on the agenda is to "Discuss the customer's needs, wants and desires". This is a great phrase that usually will put the customer at ease and does not imply that you are there to "sell" them something but you are there to help them meet their needs and wants along with the desires they might have for the company. Although this states that you are going to discuss, you are actually going to listen. Try not to talk at all during this time. Let the customer tell you what they truly want from you and what their ideas are for their company. Don't talk unless you have to. Make notes and if a question or concern comes up try to write it down to address later during the "open" spot on the list. Gather all the information you can during this period. I have gathered information that I was able to use months down the line on a call with the same customer to help close on another idea. I was able to say "Remember when you told me that you had a need for this sometime down the line? Well I have an idea that may be able to help." This section is the most important to all of them. I know that you think the recommendation and close are the important but you cannot make the correct recommendation if you don't listen or "discover" properly. This is a time to find out the "hot buttons" that the customer will respond too.

After you have discussed what the customer is actually looking for and what services you can provide, then go into your "script" and make the recommendations that you have to help the customer fulfill those needs. Shoot the moon at this point and include your highest and largest product that may even be slightly more than the customer needs. You can always sell down but it is very difficult to sell a larger product. Show the customer what you can actually do. After this be quiet and let the customer tell you how they feel about what you have just shown them. Remember to ask the customer how they feel and not what they think. Transition this into the "open" part of the agenda.

The "open" part is where you will discuss the items the customer has concerns about. This is the time for negotiations or overcoming objections. This is one of the best spots to actually sell! I will go more in depth on how to overcome objections later in the chapter. This is also the most important time to ask for the order. After you have discussed the options, ask the customer if you can write the order or the contract. You may have to go back and overcome more but ask for the sale. As I stated earlier, a large percentage of salespeople never ask for the sale.

Write the contract or order!

The "recommendation" section is for you to get leads. Ask for the customer to give you a name of three people that they think you could provide the same service that might have a similar need for a product that you can provide. This will build your network to an endless supply of new leads and income along with an endless line of sales opportunities. In the next chapter I will give you a sample referral form to use and more on this subject.

The "finalization" section is simply the time to show the customer that you stuck to their time frame and to set the next time to meet or call. (Setting the next appointment) Never leave an appointment without setting a time for the next meeting. Find out when the customer will be ready to purchase again and ask for permission to call on them again. This is another way to make sure you have a customer down the line. You always have to be building your pipeline and creating an opportunity to have business later in the month or year.

Phone

The first and foremost thing to remember when you are making a presentation over the phone is to make sure you are talking to the correct person. This can be a very costly and timely mistake. You want to talk to the decision maker, not the gatekeeper. Most, if not all companies, have a gatekeeper. Even I had one when I owned and was involved in a retail store. My manager who would answer the phone would screen the call to find out who was calling. I know that several times a sales presentation was made to her and she had no authority to make a business decision. I remember a stockbroker who made a presentation to her and told her to relate the information to me and have me call them when I was ready to buy. As you already know, all this did was waist both our times. Just make sure you are speaking with the correct person and qualify quickly to find out. If not, stop here and find out whom you need to talk to and how to get in touch with them. After you have the right person on the phone you can continue with the presentation.

There are essentially six steps to the actual script you will use instead of an agenda when you know you are making your presentation over the phone. I am not going to write your script for you, as you need to apply this to your own situation. I am going to give you the outline and approach for each area. The six stages are: Greeting to sales, questions or discovery, position, follow-up and closing.

In the greeting, this is your time to relate and as I mentioned before the time to create the expectations as to why you are there and what your agenda is. This is the time for small talk and to ease the tension if there is any. It is also a good time to make sure the customer is comfortable with you there. This is the time to build rapport with your customer. Make sure in the face-to-face situation you go ahead and ask permission to make your presentation. During this time make sure you are using your skills laid out to establish your confidence and presence along with making yourself out to be the authority figure. You should have the correct attitude and tone of voice even when you are on the phone. Just as when you are meeting in person, I make sure to dress nice. If you are sloppy in your appearance it will come across in your voice. Just as before make sure you are neat, clean and dressed nice. A little trick I learned early on is to try to smile when you are talking. Somehow the customer will know that your mood is the correct one. The sales script actually comes into play as soon as you pick up the phone to make the call. There will be interaction between you and the customer at this point. Make sure you are prepared for the call.

The second step is the questioning or "discover" phase of the script. Discover is the correct name since this is what you are trying to do during this part of the conversation. You want to listen and take notes on what the customer is trying to tell you. If the customer wants something a certain way they will let you know. This step is the second most important next to closing the sale. Listening goes along with the questioning stage. Try to ask open-ended questions that will require something other than a yes or no answer. Ask questions that are in depth and require some discussion. Make sure you are relating to the customer. Ask the question "What are your needs, wants and desires"? Remember you are trying to get all the information you can at this point so you can overcome all the objections in a few minutes and then make your recommendations. You can learn how to make and close your sale in this time frame. You should listen for key words like "finance" or "cash flow" along with when the customer is actually ready to purchase. They might be concerned with customer service or with being able to get you on the phone. Make sure you are writing down what you hear so you can go back and ask later. You do not just want to ask any questions but ask the right questions.

Positioning is a step that will take some practice. My own fault I have because of my years of experience is that I want to cut through all the small talk and get down to business. For this reason, I sometimes position early. Just as if you were making your presentation to a jury of your peers you do not want to let all your secrets out on the first statement. Make sure you have met the customer's needs and questions before you position what you want to do. I see a lot of young salespeople try to position after the greeting before even trying to find out or qualify the customer. Don't make this mistake because it can loose you more sales than you will win. The "closer" type of salesperson will try to position early. Listen, you will sometimes learn as much about yourself and sales type as you will about the customer.

Just as in the recommendation spot of a face-to-face call this is when you sit back in your chair and tell the customer "Now this is what I would like to do". This is one of the most powerful phrases I know of. Try it, it works.

In the follow up part of the call is when you ask the customer if you have answered all of their questions and concerns. Make sure you pick your battles. Make your point then move on. Don't spend too much time on a subject that only needs little attention. Make yourself out to be the authority figure. Make sure you are clear and precise in overcoming objections. Ask the customer if they have any more questions. Did you meet all their expectations? The customer will tell you. Remember, when you were in the discovery phase of the conversation, what you learned. Don't waist time on price if they told you the color was the actual problem. Listen and the follow up will come much easier. After you have made sure you have completed this stage move on to the close.

A lot of salespeople and sales classes tell you to try a soft close early in the conversation or several different closing techniques. My personal opinion is no matter what your closing technique is, just do it. That's right! Ask for the sale. It may not be the best but you have to ask in some fashion. Salespeople get all tied up in asking for the sale. They want to make sure they ask correctly. The only wrong way to ask is not to ask. My favorite closing question in the sales or leasing field is simply this "Is there any reason why you cannot sign the documents and complete the transaction today"? You would be amazed how this question will increase your close rate. This simple question made me one of the top closers in my field not to mention the money I was able to generate from it. You have to ask for the sale. I cannot stress this enough. If you fail to ask for the business you have not only let the customer down but also you let yourself down. Don't forget this is a good time to remind the customer of the F.U.D. factor. Once you have asked for the business, STOP! You have done everything correct. Don't seem pushy or anxious to complete. Let the customer have time to think. Another one of my favorite sayings is at this point after I have asked for the sale is "The next person to speak…Looses". When the customer says yes or no that is when you go to work. You cannot keep trying to close until the customer has spoken. Sometimes this is the longest point of silence. Just sit back and wait, it will be worth it.

What do you do now? Write the business!!

One of my personal things to do when the contract is signed is to congratulate the customer on there decision. Continue to make the customer feel good about what they have just done and the decision they have just made. You will be amazed at how far this will take you. Make the customer feel important. They are. Remember if it were not for the customer you would not have a job or a source of income. You cannot stop here. After you have the confidence of the customer it is time to ask for recommendations. Again, I will go much more in-depth later in the chapter, but it is an important part of the sales process. As I mentioned before, this is how you establish future business and create a pipeline or forecast for later on. The simplest and easiest way to ask is to see if the customer has someone in mind, possibly a person or business mentioned in the discovery section that you might be able to offer the same type of assistance or service that you just provided to them. You can help the customer to feel proud of their choice and let their friends and co-workers know that they are on top of things. Try to get at least 3 referrals from the customer. If you can do this on every call even if you cannot make a sale on every call you can assure yourself that you will be very busy over the upcoming months making presentations and contacts. You will never run out of people to tell your story to.

Last, but not least, make sure you ask for the chance to call on the customer again in the future. Always find a time when you can either make a face-to-face appointment or another time to call. You will want to try to make every customer a repeat customer even if you cannot get a commitment for an exact time to call. Do it anyway. If nothing else call and just follow up with what the customer just purchased from you. Don't let another sales person in the door.

Secret to closing the sale

I have already given you the first secret. The most important secret to closing business is simply to ask for it. I gave the fact earlier that 63% of all sales end without the salesperson asking for the business. This is terrible. How can you expect a customer to purchase from you if you never ask them to purchase. I relayed a story earlier about the girl who set next to me for a while that could not understand what she was doing wrong. She made a great presentation giving all the proper closes except she never asked for the business. (Sales is offer and acceptance if no offer is made how can potential buyers accept?) The second most important part or secret actually comes before you ask for the sale. This secret is overcoming objections.

Tom Hopkins once made a statement that "All buyers feel and act on the urge to say no at first". Think about this, over 50% of all sales will require you to **overcome** one or more **objections**. Overcoming objections is one of the key strategies of all sales. If you cannot overcome objections you will not become great and ultimately fail in the sales industry. Failure to overcome every objection will equal no sale. Your presentation and attitude can be perfect and you may be one of the best at creating a rapport with the customer but if you cannot deal correctly with objections you cannot be effective. When you properly overcome an objection several things start to happen. The first thing is you immediately gain credibility and migrate closer to finalizing the process. You will also create a sense of satisfaction with the customer that you actually care about their concern. Every time you overcome one of the customers's objections or concerns make sure they agree that you took care of their need. This will help later when you are making your presentation. Some people call this a soft close. (Make sure you ask the customer in the correct way.) Ask the customer how they feel rather than what they think. Don't forget that most purchases are done on emotions. Use this to your advantage.

Make sure that you understand what the customer is asking of you. Also make sure that you understand the difference between a simple question and an objection. Is the customer making a statement or is the customer actually objecting to something. There are several different ways to try to relate to the customer and an actual process to overcoming objections. One of the oldest and most used as well as taught is the Feel, Felt, Found method.

You need to be very careful as sometimes this comes across as being fake or insensitive. I know of almost as many sales lost with this method as they are gained. Simply put you can relate this method to almost any situation. This is the catch phrase involved in Feel, Felt, and Found. "I can appreciate how you FEEL, other people I have worked with initially FELT the same way too until they FOUND after meeting with me that … (restate the benefit) … I'd like to see if we can do the same for you. With that in mind would… (Offer choices from objection)". Again, this method will work on most people but be careful. With me being an experienced sales person, when another person starts this phrase with me, I instantly shut them out. They just lost my business because I feel that I am going to be "sold". In the insurance business, the great follow up to getting an appointment was to use this phrase followed by "Let me show you how through meeting with me I can increase your net worth, decrease your taxes and increase your spendable income". You would be crazy not to meet with that person if they can do this. And you can do this with several different insurance products. You have done several things here not only did you divert the true objection but you were able to create an interest in another benefit. Dale Carnegie came up with a great modification to this phrase that I personally like to use from time to time. He uses empathy with the customer in modifying the statement to " I understand how you FEEL, I would FEEL the same way in your situation, let's see if we can find a solution to your concern" notice that this whole statement is based on emotion. You must show true concerns and find the hot buttons that enable you to work towards the close of the sale. Another major mistake I see new sales people make is to make the statement "to tell you the truth". They are actually trying to show empathy towards the customer but this is the wrong way to do it. When you make a statement like "to tell you the truth" this implies that up until this point you have been lying to the customer. You do not want to say or do anything that will lower your credibility. The next time a person makes this statement to you ask them if up until this time they have been lying to you and see the response you will get.

Generally, there is a simple process to overcoming objections and as long as you follow these simple steps you will do fine. You can use any of the suggestions or methods above but just make sure to do these things.

First make sure you listen to the question or objection and then repeat it back to the customer to make sure you understand exactly what the customer is asking of you. Next thank the customer for bringing this to your attention. Yes, you read this correctly. Thank the customer for making an objection. Show empathy to the objection. "A lot of other people felt the same way as you". Then simply overcome the objection or answer the question. Make your statement or show your benefit and how it can solve the problem. Last, ask the customer if this meets their need. Did you overcome and answer their question? Make the customer state "Yes that answers my question". You will need to remind the customer that you did this later. If the customer states that your answer does not overcome their objection then simply start over on the process from the top.

Tom Harmon's theory is that "If you fail to overcome an objection the first time raised…. Your chances for success go down to 50% or less". Make sure you know how to accomplish this. Develop your own style with the above methods to successfully and constantly overcome the customer's objections. As equally important, if you do not know the answers to the question or concern tell the customer that you will find out the answer. Then go and find the answer. Maintain your credibility. Again, a sale is offer and acceptance. Your offer may be overcoming an objection or presenting a solution to the customer's concerns.

A sale is completed, when you have a check in your hand. Not when you are through with your presentation.

Until you have a funding source, someone else can come along and get your customer. You have done it to other salespeople and they can do it to you. If you require a follow up to pick up a check or signed agreement make sure you are there. It is more import to keep a two-minute appointment to pick up a check than it is to keep a one-hour appointment presentation to a new customer. Don't get me wrong both are equally as important but until you have the money in your hand you don't have a sale. Not to be cheesy, but I believe someone once stated that "A bird in the hand is better than two in the bush". Something to think about.

Referrals or recommendations

I have made the statement several times so far that the very last thing you need to do is ask for referrals or recommendations. This is one of the best but most forgotten aspects of a call. There are not many instances where you as a salesperson are presented with an endless supply of people to talk to. Unless you are in a captive situation with a manufacturer and even then you will still need to hunt new calls.

At the end of the meeting, if in person, I like to take out 3 business cards or better yet possibly a brochure on my company or product. I will then ask the customer that has just purchased from me to write one sentence saying that I was able to help them with a need and thought he could do the same for you. Then get the names of three close people that the customer believes will have the same needs, wants and desires as they do.

Explain to the customer that you will send the referral a letter simply stating that I had met with the customer and their name was mentioned as a person who could benefit from my services. I like to use a simple one-paragraph form letter and take a copy with me to show the customer. Make the customer feel important as well as comfortable with what you are doing. State in the letter that within the next week you will be calling to see when the best time would be to discuss how and what you can do for them. When you call the customer they should already know who you are and why you are calling as well as have a hand written sentence from a friend of theirs that you were able to help. You cannot imagine the magnitude this will have on the referred customer. I don't ever remember not getting an appointment with a person or company when it was referred to me in this manner. If by some chance when you call the customer and don't get an appointment make sure and ask for permission to call on them in the future. I will show you how to keep track of these leads later on. When you send out your referral letter make sure you put either the business card or brochure with the customer's comments in the letter.

The customer will sometimes state that they cannot think of anyone to refer to you. Give them examples of friends, family, co-workers, knitting group, lodge members or social groups as well as their religious organization or church. Everyone knows at least three people. This whole process should only take a few minutes and at the first of your face-to-face presentation you already set the expectation that you would be asking later in the conversation.

If you are making the phone presentation, you can basically ask in the same way except to have the customer write something for you. Ask the customer for a person or business that they feel could benefit from your product or service. As soon as you hang up the phone one of the referrals should be your very next call. Start the conversation by stating that you just got off the phone with a mutual friend and tell them whom it was. All you are doing in this call is getting permission to either call them again at a better time or go ahead and set a face-to-face appointment. If you can set the appointment, this is the best thing but it is not always this easy. Even if the customer will not let you call or set an appointment go ahead and send them a letter thanking them for talking with you and to let them know how to contact you if they find they need your assistance later on. This puts you one step ahead of the competition or the next person calling. They will remember you if you follow these steps. By utilizing this lead or referral process you will be able to manage your 10-3-1 rule more effectively as well as establish a never ending list of prospects. The whole process is just having people to talk to on a daily basis.

Closing tools

A closing tool is nothing more than your offer to entice the customer to purchase from you. Most everyone understands what a closing tool is but not how to use it effectively. The proper way to use a closing tool is to offer the customer something in exchange for something else. My favorite and the most common in my field is an issue of interest rate. So, if this objection comes up and I need to lower the rate I will but I will make the statement "If I can get this rate lower, can you make the purchase and sign the agreement today?" Make sure that the customer understands that a closing tool is just that. Not something thrown into the deal as an extra but an offer to help entice the customer to move or "pull the trigger" on the transaction within a given time. This will also help to re-establish the F.U.D. factor and ultimately close the sale now and not tomorrow. If you have a special promotion or discount available that you need to pull out to help with the sale make sure that it is understood that the only way you can make the offer is if the customer can give you a commitment as to when you can finalize the transaction. Don't give away the farm just because you can or have a certain tool available. I assure you that if you discount an item by 10% the customer will ask for 15%. (Ask during the closing and checking stage of the conversation what it will take to get the customers business.) Let the customer tell you and then try to accomplish and beat their expectations if possible. This for that, give and take, offer and acceptance none of which this is for nothing or offer and offer again, get something back in return for your closing tool and use it accordingly. Remember what the offers are for. They are there to help you close business not to lower your profit or gain on the sale. Not to mention your personal commission or pay.

Chapter 4
Types of customers and people

1. Color test
2. Ready buyers
3. Tire kickers
4. Information gatherers
5. No prospects

I want to take this chapter to discuss different types of customers and people. Now that you have the understanding of how to make a presentation you also must understand the differences between "color types" and how to recognize these easily. The first thing you must do is understand what color type you are first and how you are perceived by other colors. I am sure you are asking yourself what's all this "color" stuff? Back several years ago, a gentleman by the name of Taylor Hartman, PH.D., developed a personality profile to determine and assign a number that in turn is assigned by a color. There are four basic colors: red, blue, white, and yellow. After you find out what color you are he gave a list of characteristics of that color type. You are probably wondering what this has to do with sales. Well this has everything to do with sales. You must be able to understand what type of person and pick up on the traits of each individual to better understand what they might feel or to better understand how and what would be the best approach to them.

Dr. Hartman made the statement "We are most effective in understanding other people when we see them whole---treating them as complete personalities rather than focusing on either their strengths or limitations." If I had been shown this at an earlier age I know that it could have influenced my ability to exchange ideas and information better with potential customers.

Below you will find the "color test". Please take it, if only for fun to see how you relate to other colors. You will find it amazingly accurate and I know the first time I took it I was shocked at how the information related to me as a person and also a sales person. You should choose one of the answers either a, b, c or d that best describes you as a person.

Strengths and limitations

1. a) Opinionated
   b) Nurturing
   c) Inventive
   d) Outgoing

2. a) Power-oriented
   b) Perfectionist
   c) Indecisive
   d) Self-centered

3. a) Dominant
   b) Sympathetic
   c) Tolerant
   d) Enthusiastic

4. a) Self-serving
   b) Suspicious
   c) Unsure
   d) Naïve

5. a) Decisive
   b) Loyal
   c) Content
   d) Playful

6. a) Arrogant
   b) Worry prone
   c) Silently stubborn
   d) Flighty

7. a) Assertive
   b) Reliable
   c) Kind
   d) Sociable

8. a) Bossy
   b) Self-critical
   c) Reluctant
   d) A teaser

9. a) Action-oriented
   b) Analytical
   c) Easygoing
   d) Carefree

10. a) Critical of others
    b) Overly sensitive
    c) Shy
    d) Obnoxious

11. a) Determined
    b) Detail conscious
    c) A good listener
    d) A party person

12. a) Demanding
    b) Unforgiving
    c) Unmotivated
    d) Vain

13. a) Responsible
    b) Idealistic
    c) Considerate
    d) Happy

14. a) Impatient
    b) Moody
    c) Passive
    d) Impulsive

15. a) Strong-willed
    b) Respectful
    c) Patient
    d) Fun-loving

16. a) Argumentative
    b) Unrealistic
    c) Directionless
    d) An interrupter

17. a) Independent
    b) Dependable
    c) Even-tempered
    d) Trusting

18. a) Aggressive
    b) Frequently depressed
    c) Ambivalent
    d) Forgetful

19. a) Powerful
    b) Deliberate
    c) Gentle
    d) Optimistic

20. a) Insensitive
    b) Judgmental
    c) Boring
    d) Undisciplined

21.a) Logical
   b) Emotional
   c) Agreeable
   d) Popular

22. a) Always right
    b) Guilt prone
    c) Unenthusiastic
    d) Uncommitted

23.a) Pragmatic
   b) Well-behaved
   c) Accepting
   d) Spontaneous

24. a) Merciless
    b) thoughtful
    c) Uninvolved
    d) A show-off

25.a) Task-oriented
   b) Sincere
   c) Diplomatic
   d) Lively

26. a) Tactless
    b) Hard to Please
    c) Lazy
    d) Loud

27.a) Direct
   b) Creative
   c) Adaptable
   d) A performer

28. a) Calculating
    b) Self-righteous
    c) Self-deprecating
    d) Disorganized

29. a) Confident
    b) Disciplined
    c) Pleasant
    d) Charismatic

30. a) Intimidating
    b) Careful
    c) Unproductive
    d) Afraid to face facts

Strengths and limitations Totals

___Total a's   ___Total b's   ___Total c's   ___Total d's

Enter your totals in the proper spaces. Now let's see if you respond the same way to the following situation as you did to groups of descriptive words. Again, pick only one answer, and record your totals for each letter at the end of the section.

Situations

31. If I applied for a job, a prospective employer would most likely hire me because I am:
    a) Driven, direct and delegating
    b) Deliberate, accurate and reliable
    c) Patient, adaptable and tactful
    d) Fun-loving, spirited and casual

32. When involved in an intimate relationship, if I feel threatened by my partner, I:
    a) Fight back with facts and anger
    b) Cry, feel hurt, and plan revenge
    c) Become quiet, withdrawn, and often hold anger until I blow up over some minor issue
    d) Distance myself and avoid further conflict

33. For me, like is most meaningful when it:
    a) Is task-oriented and productive
    b) Is filled with people and purpose
    c) Is free of pressure and stress
    d) Allows me to be playful, lighthearted and optimistic

34. As a child, I was;
    a) Stubborn, bright and or aggressive
    b) Well-behaved, caring and or depressed
    c) Quite, easygoing and or shy
    d) Too talkative, happy and or playful

35. As an adult, I am:
    a) Opinionated, determined and or bossy
    b) Responsible, honest and or unforgiving
    c) Accepting, content and or unmotivated
    d) Charismatic, positive and or obnoxious

36. As a parent I am:
    a) Demanding, quick-tempered and or uncompromising
    b) Concerned, sensitive and or critical
    c) Permissive, easily persuaded and or often overwhelmed
    d) Playful, casual and or irresponsible

37. In an argument with a friend I am most likely to be:
    a) Verbally stubborn about facts
    b) Concerned about others feelings and principles
    c) Silently stubborn, uncomfortable and or confused
    d) Loud, uncomfortable and or compromising

38. If my friend were in trouble I would be:
    a) Protective, resourceful and recommend solutions

b) Concerned, empathetic and loyal regardless or the problem
c) Supportive, patient and a good listener
d) Nonjudgmental, optimistic and down-playing the seriousness of the situation

39. When making decisions I am:
a) Assertive, articulate and logical
b) Deliberate, precise and cautious
c) Indecisive, timid and reluctant
d) Impulsive, uncommitted and inconsistent

40. When I fail I feel:
a) Silently self-critical yet verbally stubborn and defensive
b) Guilty, self-critical and vulnerable to depression
c) Unsettled and fearful but I keep it to myself
d) Embarrassed and nervous seeking to escape the situation

41. If someone crosses me:
a) I am angered and cunningly plan ways to get even quickly
b) I feel deeply hurt and find it almost impossible to forgive completely generally getting even is not enough
c) I am silently hurt an plan to get even and or completely avoid the other person
d) I want to avoid confrontation, consider the situation not important enough to bother with and or seek other friends

42. Work is:
    a) A most productive way to spend one's time
    b) A healthy activity, which should be done right if it's to be done at all
    c) A positive activity as long as it is something I enjoy and don't feel pressured to do
    d) A necessary evil, much less inviting than play

43. In social situation I am most often:
    a) Feared by others
    b) Admired by others
    c) Protected by others
    d) Envied by others

44. In a relationship I am most concerned with being:
    a) Approved of and right
    b) Understood, appreciated and intimate
    c) Respected, tolerant and peaceful
    d) Praised, having fun and feeling free

45. To feel alive and positive I seek:
    a) Adventure, leadership and lots of action
    b) Security, creative and purpose
    c) Acceptance and safety
    d) Excitement, playful productivity and the company of others

Situation totals

___ Total a's ___ Total b's ___ Total c's ___ Total d's

Now add your totals from numbers 1-30 to those from numbers 31-45 to get a grand total. At this point, the four personality color types are assigned to each of the letters: Red for "a", Blue for "b", White for "c" and Yellow for "d".

Grand totals

___ Red "a" ___ Blue "b" ___ White "c" ___ Yellow "d"

Now that you know what color type you are, the next section will give basic characteristics of the different colors along with do's and don'ts on how to relate to each. See how your color fits with the chart. I know with my own experience I was pleasantly surprised as well as informed as to why I sometimes respond and act in a certain way.

	Red	Blue	White	Yellow
Motive:	Power	Intimacy	Peace	Fun
Needs:	To look good	To be good	To feel good	To look good
	To be right	To be understood	To be allowed their own space	To be noticed
	To be respected	To be appreciated	To be respected	To be praised

	Approval from A select few	Acceptance	Tolerance	Approval from the masses
Wants:	To Hide Insecurities Tightly	To reveal insecurities	To withhold insecurities	To hide insecurities loosely
	Productivity	Quality	Kindness	Happiness
	Leadership	Autonomy	Independence	Freedom
	Challenging adventure	Security	Contentment	Playful adventure

See if these truly match up to your emotions and feelings. The next section is how one color will relate to another color.

How to develop a positive connection with reds:

Do:
1. Present issues logically
2. Demand their attention and respect
3. Do your homework
4. Be direct, brief, and specific in conversation
5. Be productive and efficient
6. Offer them leadership opportunities
7. Verbalize your feelings
8. Support their decisive nature
9. Promote their intelligent reasoning where appropriate
10. Be prepared with facts and figures

11. Respect their need to make their own decisions their own way

Don't:
1. Embarrass them in front of others
2. Argue from an emotional perspective
3. Always use authoritarian approach
4. Use physical punishment
5. Be slow and indecisive
6. Expect a personal and intimate relationship
7. Attack them personally
8. Take their arguments personally
9. Wait for them to solicit your opinion
10. Demand constant social interaction (allow for alone time)

How to develop a positive connection with blues:

Do:
1. Emphasize their security in the relationship
2. Be sensitive and soft-spoken in your approach
3. Be sincere and genuine
4. Behave appropriately and well mannered
5. Limit their risk level
6. Allow ample time for them to gather their thoughts before expressing themselves
7. Appreciate them
8. Promote their creativity
9. Be loyal
10. Do thorough analysis before making presentations

Don't:
1. Make them feel guilty
2. Be rude or abrupt
3. Promote too much change
4. Expect spontaneity
5. Abandon them
6. Expect them to bounce back easily or quickly from depression
7. Demand perfection (they already expect too much from themselves)
8. Push them too quickly into making decisions

How to develop a positive connection with whites:

Do:
1. Be kind
2. Be logical, clear and firm about the content you present
3. Provide a structure (boundaries) for them to operate in
4. Be patient and gentle
5. Introduce options and ideas for their involvement
6. Be simple and open
7. Acknowledge and accept their individuality
8. Be casual, informal and relaxed in presentation style
9. Look for nonverbal clues to their feelings
10. Listen quietly

Don't:
1. Be cruel or insensitive
2. Expect them to need much social interaction
3. Force immediate verbal expression; accept written communication
4. Be domineering or too intense
5. Demand conformity to unrealistic expectations, behaviors
6. Overwhelm them with too much at once
7. Force confrontation
8. Speak to fast
9. Take away all their daydreams
10. Demand leadership

How to develop a positive relationship with yellows:

Do:
1. Be positive and proactive with them in your life
2. Adore and praise them legitimately
3. Touch them physically
4. Accept their playful teasing
5. Remember they are more sensitive than they appear
6. Value their social interaction skills and people connections
7. Remember they hold feelings deeply
8. Promote creative and fun activities for and with them
9. Enjoy their charismatic innocence
10. Allow them opportunity for verbal expression

Don't:
1. Be too serious or sober in criticism
2. Push them too intensely
3. Ignore them
4. Forget they have "down" time also
5. Demand perfection
6. Expect them to dwell on problems
7. Give them too much rope; or they may hang themselves
8. Classify them as a lightweight social butterflies
9. Attack their sensitivity or be unforgiving
10. Totally control their schedules or consume their time

After you have taken some time with these, make sure you try to understand the differences between color types and how they can relate to your particular sales type and the type you are trying to maintain in your sales environment. If you can become familiar with the different types and how you should approach these types when making a presentation you have all the ammunition you could possibly handle. As you see, this could be a great advantage in your sales approach. I wish I would have known about Dr. Hartman's color test earlier in my sales career. I can see where utilizing this information would and could have been a great benefit to closing deals. Dr. Hartman has written several books detailing and going much further in depth on the color test. I would advise you to read these as an accurate source of information on this subject as I have only given you a brief look at the understanding of his great work.

This is one of those areas that I try to go back and review every few months because I feel if you can better understand people, you will better understand where a customer is coming from and this will ultimately help you in your career, not only with customers but with your peers and also your managers or if you are a manger it will help with how to deal with your employees.

When I owned the Tobacco stores, I had at one time around 12 employees each with a different personality and color type. After getting to know each in his or her own way I was a better manager because I was able to understand what motivated each. This created a better manager employee relationship because we now understood each other and started to work together rather than against one another.

The color test is also a great tool to use in your marriage or relationship to better understand the needs of another color. When my wife took the test I quickly realized some of the things I may have been doing wrong and started to study how to do it correctly.

Buying types: Ready buyers

As we look at the different types of buyers or customers we try to examine not only where the customer is in regards to being ready to purchase from you but also if the customer has the resources to complete the sale. I have dealt with hundreds of customer that were "ready buyers" except for the funding source. Either they did not have the funds or could not get approved to borrow the funds.

The "ready buyer" is the buyer or customer you could deal with on every call. This customer has met all the criteria and is your best prospect. It is essential in the sales process to understand where your customer is. I have found that the "ready buyer" is the one that is the most fun to deal with and usually is open to suggestions. What makes a "ready buyer" and what do you need to do to win the business?

A "ready buyer", as I mentioned, has met certain criteria. Not only have they decided to buy but they also have a funding source and have the money to be able to purchase now. The "ready buyer" has already made up their mind that they are going to purchase the product. It is up to you to make sure that they purchase from you. In most cases, the "ready buyer" will not require much in the way of selling to. They have already sold themselves and sometimes know as much about the product as the person selling.

You will still have to overcome objections and try to build rapport with the customer. Just because they are ready to purchase they have not committed to you as the one they want to purchase from. About the only thing you can do different in your presentation is talk less. The more you talk to the "ready buyer" the more chance of losing the sale.

Once you have made the understanding that the customer you are presenting to is the "ready buyer" it is at this point that you make sure that the customer buys from you and not someone else.

The next type of buyer is the "tire kicker" or shopper. The biggest difference between the "tire kicker" and the "ready buyer" is time. The "tire kicker" has decided to purchase. They are just not ready yet. Of course the name "tire kicker" came from years ago in the car business when a customer would kick the tire of a car to determine the quality and check the air. In essence when you are confronted with the "tire kicker" you need to be the tire kicker sales person.

The tire kicker sales person is the one that continues to ask questions in an effort to find out what the true objection is with respect to time. "Tire kickers" can easily be turned into "ready buyers" with the right presentation. This is the second most active buyer. They are already sold on the product and again usually have already made up their mind to purchase. Either time or the funding source is not quite ready.

If time is an issue you should be able to create F.U.D to help overcome this but if funding is the issue you either need to have an idea of another funding source or follow up at the time you think the funding source is ready. I recently went to a Flea Market with an uncle of mine. We were watching a demonstration where a lady was showing us one of those choppers with the crank on the top. My uncle was slightly interested in the product but at this point it was just a spontaneous issue. He tried to say no and use the "tire kicker" approach stating that he only had a credit card. The lady quickly responded with "I bet your friend (referring to me) has $20 you can borrow and then you can just pay him back". What the lady had just done was overcome an objection and locate an alternate funding source. My uncle bought the chopper and I bet that it has never been out of the box. He has also not gone back to the Flea Market with me. We still laugh at the story. Just as in any case, someone is going to get sold it is either you or the customer. In this incident, it was us the customer. I would dare to say that the lady selling the choppers did not have any kind of formal sales classes but she was able to think quickly and therefore close the sale. We were serious shoppers or "tire kickers" whose concerns and objections were quickly overcome and moved into the spot of a "ready buyer". This is your goal with all tire kickers.

Information gatherers are those customers that have not yet decided to purchase but are trying to get enough information to purchase soon or decide whether or not to purchase at all. The strongest thing about the "information gatherers" is the fact that they are interested in the product and they are talking to you. Although the customer has not yet decided to purchase they can be moved to becoming a "tire kicker" quickly. I told you earlier in the book about my wife and I looking for a video camera. We were "information gatherers" at this point. Unless you are really good at what you do your best chance with an "information gatherers" is after they have already talked to someone else and have a little knowledge about the product.

When you are dealing with the "information gatherers", use broad terms to establish the amount of knowledge the customer has about the product. Just as when I was talking to the camera person that was a "techie" sales type; he talked over my head and thus turned me off and I purchased from another vendor. Show the big details and use general terms like, roomy or compact, economy model or top of the line. These types of questions will help to establish what color type and what the customer's true concerns are.

When talking to the "information gatherers" stick to the subject of the product. Sell the customer on the product and make sure to build the rapport we have discussed several times. Over the weekend my wife and I needed to look for a new refrigerator. We were somewhat "information gatherers" and also "tire kickers". We already had an interest in the product but needed more information and also needed to gather this information in order to get the funding source together. At the store, the sales lady quickly approached us from the standpoint of the product and nothing else. She gave us benefits and helped us to gather information and allowed us to leave without being too pushy. We went home and established the funding source and called in the order and purchased the fridge the sales lady had shown us. We went through several different customer types in just a matter of hours.

When dealing with the "information gatherers", sell them on the product then quickly move them onto the timing of there purchase and if they leave make sure they know how to get in touch with you when they are ready to move forward. You have shown that you are the authority figure and the customer should call you when they have questions.

The **negative prospect** is possibly the hardest customer type to deal with but worth taking the time to make a presentation to. There are going to be one of three types of negative prospects. The not interested, the customer who already has a similar product and is happy with what they have and the customer who has owned the product in the past but was not satisfied with it. The negative prospect is the customer who has reluctantly given you five minutes to make a twenty-minute presentation.

I was cold calling on a small high school in East Texas around the first of May, just before school was out, to see about doing the school's summer instrument repair. Of course I had called ahead and set up a time with the band director in an effort to try to establish a warm customer call. I arrived at the school on time and met the director whom eagerly accepted my presence. The director listened to my presentation. I had visual aids and pictures to make a good 15 or 20 minute speech. We quickly established a quick relationship and the customer took me as someone trying to help him and not sell him. Things were going well. The director invited me to lunch in the school cafeteria and on the way told me that he would be happy to send a few instruments with me but would first have to clear it through his principle. This was a common practice so I did not think anything of it. At lunch we happened to sit directly across from his principle. He introduced me and explained who I was and that he wanted to take advantage of my services. The principle looked at me and then looked at his director and in a stern voice asked that we meet him in his office after lunch. I went into the office with my presentation in hand ready for a few minutes of my pitch. The principle looked at me and the first thing he asked was "Mr. Fielder, do you have a tie with you?" I told him that I had a tie in my car and would be happy to get it. The principle made me go to my car and put a tie on before he would listen to me. When I got back, he informed me that I had exactly 4 minutes to tell him why I was there and show him how I could save his school money. I changed my 20 minute presentation into a 3 ½-minute sales pitch and left the office. I was not happy with what had just happened but continued with the process. The principle talked to his director and then asked me to come back into his office at which point he told me that I could take up to $40,000 dollars worth of repair and anything over that he could not pay for. Somehow I got the business and left knowing where I stood and what to expect. The next time I went back to the school, I made sure I had on a tie and over the next 2 years I did a little over $250,000 worth of repair. This is a perfect example of how a negative prospect can quickly change. There was nothing positive about this customer except the fact that they did allow me to do the business.

With a negative prospect, you have to find the real objection and then move onto the serious buyer. If you cannot, stop. Don't sit on china eggs. Look for the real reasons the customer is not interested. In my case it had nothing to do with a tie or a presentation. The customer just wanted to know how I was going to save him money over the long run. I was able to show him and overcome his objection and therefore save the sale. I have made presentations out in freshly plowed fields and even on top of a building. This is one of the reasons I was and continue to be successful. I always try to find out what the customer's true needs are and then set out to meet them.

Chapter 5
Tools and Plans

1. Lead, Call box
2. Out bounding
3. Thank you letters
4. Goals
5. Financial Plan
6. Mentors

In this section I want to go in depth on a more personal nature. Along with a few more essential tools that will help you in your everyday sales plan, I also want to discuss a few subjects that will help in your personal plan. Being in sales is a great profession however; if not careful you can let it take over your life. I know of people who live and breathe sales to a point that it is the only thing on their mind. You must be able to organize your day and month to allow you ample time for other things besides your job or the call you don't want to miss tomorrow. There is a simple way to organize your time in a little box of cards. I did not come across the card box until later in my career but I quickly saw how helpful it would have been when I was on the road. I call it a Lead or Call box.

The lead or call box is nothing more than a way to keep up with calls and sometimes appointments. You will need some supplies for this and I strongly encourage you to try this. It will only cost you a few dollars to get it started and you should see results from the first time you use it. Go to the store and get these items:

1. Recipe box for 4 x 5 index cards
2. Package of 4 x 5 index cards
3. At least 70 dividers that stick out above the cards

That's it. That is all you will need to start one of the most valuable sales tools known to man. Here is how you set up your card box.

First, create a divider for each day of the month and put these in the front of the box. Second, create a divider for each month. Third, create a spot for each letter of the alphabet. Fourth, create a divider in the back of the box for misc. or other.

Now your box is set up. Next you need to create what information you need on your index cards. I suggest that you use the sample below and try to modify it to your best situation. I like this form of a card because it is not only simple but also easy to locate information on the card. Whatever type of card you use make sure that you use the same format for each and everyone. You will be handling these a lot so make sure you keep them accurate. You will also want to make sure and carry several blank cards along with you and keep your call box close when you are making a new call.

The card:

Name of account: **Date:**
Account #   Call back date:
Contact name
Business Address
Home Address
Business structure: LLC, Inc, Sole prop, other
Phone: ext.
Home phone
Fax
E-mail address
Any credit notes:
Notes:

Okay, this is simple so far. It is not just the card but how you use it. On every call either in person or on the phone, make out one of these cards. I feel like the most important information is in the date to call back spot and the notes section. After the call, make a quick statement about what you talked about and what the customer wanted you to do. Next, mark the date when the customer wants you to call them back. That's all the information you will need on the cards.

The rest of this section is how to organize the cards and sort them to be helpful to you. After you make out a card and find out the date when the customer will want you to call, you will get one of two things. Either the customer will want you to call back later in the month or they will want you to call back some months later possibly next quarter or at a six month follow up. This is where the box comes in. If the customer states to you to call back next Thursday then you simply file the card along with the information from the call and why you need to call them (don't rely on your memory) in the file that corresponds to the date for next Thursday. If the customer asks you to call them next month sometime then you go to the months file in your box and put this card in the corresponding month.

Here is how to make it work for you. Every day the first thing in the morning or ideally the night before just when you are finishing up your day, go to the box and take out all the cards for that day that you have filed in the past. You will have everything you need to be able to make sure you call the customer when you and the client agreed for you to call. This will be most impressive to the customer when you call that you not only called on time but you were able to bring up in the conversation why you are calling and that the customer had asked you to.

At the first of each month you go to that month in your file box and go through all the cards where customers asked you to call in the month and place each card in the correct day file when you need to contact them.

Remember that the days of the month are only for current calls that month. With this system you will always be on top of the call and the contact. The alphabet section in the back of the box are for customers that do not require a set follow up but you need to maintain a card on them. If you receive a call from one of these customers you can easily go to the box and pull up the information you have so it will be right in front of you while you are talking to the customer.

In today's world of computers and programs with e-mail you can utilize some of these same practices on your computer.

I use a program at work that allows me to view and save appointments or task months or even years in advance. I will go to the day I need to call a customer back and then set it to remind me the day before or the morning of the call. This works great but you are not always at your computer or online in the case of a desktop when you are on an outside call. I always carry my call box with me and in the very least the blank cards or the cards of the people that I need to contact that day.

I had a salesperson that was a stockbroker that would call me from time to time when I owned the stores in Corpus Christi. He must of used the card box because every time I would tell him to call me in a week or call me a month from Monday he would call right on the dot. He never missed a call. I even started marking it on my calendar to see if he would call when he said he would. He always did and the other thing that I always found interesting is that he also would start the conversation right where we left off the last time. This was a great selling tool and I could instantly see how effective this was.

If I would have had and used this system when I was on the road I would have never missed a call. I would use sticky notes and put them in a line across the dash of my suburban of when I needed to call a customer. I think you can tell that this would have been a better system to use. I was in a sales environment once that used this system religiously and it became a game to see which one of us would have a bigger stack of cards each morning tucked away in our front shirt pocket.

Out bounding

Michael Hall in my job interview asked me what I thought the most important thing about sales was. I am not sure of what my response was but I remember what his was and have thought about it often. Michael's statement was "Out bounding is to sales as location is to real estate". What a powerful statement. Let me clarify out bounding. Out bounding is the process of following up on a sales call after you have completed the presentation. In a lot of cases the customer will be left to make a decision or a time frame to complete the sale. Even if you were in a business like car sales or insurance sales, out bounding would be a great addition to your sales tools. Has a car salesperson ever called you back after you went and visited to take a test drive? Probably not, just think about the impact this could have on a customer if a simple call to see if the customer had the chance to discuss what and how they felt about their test drive.

Michael's statement about real estate, I am sure you have heard several times, "Location, location, and location". You can have a great house that is in a bad neighborhood and only get a fraction of what it is worth if it were a somewhat bad house in a great location. Michael's simple analogy is one that stresses how important out bounding is in the sales process. This is a funny subject that Michael and I have had several discussions about. When I first worked for him I had the lowest out bound number of any of his reps however, I had the number one close rate. My argument was that if you close the customer on the first call you could eliminate the need for the outbound follow up. What I found out is that if I would out bound to the remainder of the customers that I was unable to close quickly I could increase my close rate by another one or two percent. I know that one or two percent does not sound like much but over a years time it made a tremendous effect on the bottom line.

Now, we cannot forget that out bounding must be done correctly. If you are going to make the effort to outbound make sure you are out bounding to close the deal. I told the story earlier in the book about the girl that would do all the out bounds but never ask for the business when she did them. This is a simple tool that can make a huge difference and put you over the top in the view of your peers. There is a direct correlation between out bounds and the number of closes. There is no way you can call

all the customers that you failed to close on the first presentation and not close more business.

I quickly found out that a lot of the time when I would get into the second or even the third call on a big deal the objection was just a misunderstanding or confusion. I remember I was working with a customer on a fairly large deal and on the third call I realized that his only objection that he had was not including the tax on his monthly payment. After explaining where and what the tax was, he was great with the contract and signed it that very moment with me on the phone. If I had not made that third call I would not have closed the business. It did not take me long to realize once again I still had something to learn about the sales business.

Thank you letters

Thank you letters are another way of follow up to a visit. The best thank you letter story was from a sailboat shop in Austin, Texas. I was on the road back in about 1992 or summer of '93 and my travels brought me to Austin. I was in the market for a sailboat and went to a local shop I had spotted. I was greeted by a friendly salesperson who I chatted with for a while discussing what type and style of boat I was looking for. We spent about an hour together talking about boats and what I did and where I lived. Before I left, he asked me if he could get some information from me so he would have a record of my visit. Being in sales, myself, I thought nothing of this and thus gave him my name and address along with my phone number. It was about a week later I checked my mailbox to find a thank you card.

The card was a very simple white card and blank on the inside where the salesperson that I had spent time with had written these simple words: "Mr. Fielder, it was nice to see you in our store and your interest in a sailboat. I enjoyed talking to you and I hope in the future when you are ready to get into a new boat you will give me a call. I hope your music career continues to prosper." This was the first hand written personalized thank you I have ever received. To this day, I still remember that. It made a great impression on me.

I set out to make this same impression on people as well. If you are in the large ticket item sales, the use of a thank you note is a great relationship tool. Let me tell you about my friend, Raymond. I had only been on the phones for months at Dell Financial when I had a gym owner by the name of Raymond inquire about a lease. The transaction was only about $1200 but I treated it as if it was for $100,000. The call required a follow-up call and Raymond and I ended up speaking several times the same day trying to complete the transaction. After the sale was all done and about a week later I called him just to check and see if he had received his computer and if everything was okay. He was so impressed with the fact that I took time to call and thank him as well as make sure his system arrived in time that we quickly became friends. Raymond has never bought another item from me but has referred several customers to me. To this day, he will call just to check and see how things are going. Last week he called me because he had seen on the news that several Dell employees had been laid off and he wanted to make sure that I was okay and made the cut. I would take 100 customers and friends like Raymond any day and I hope that the relationship started because I was able to do my job at a superior level. I have never met Raymond face to face but the next time I am in his state I will make sure and go by to see him in person.

The reason I tell you this story is to better understand how relationships and emotions continue to be the driving force in sales. If you can make a friend you can make a customer for life. But as I also learned early in my career if you think that the customer is a friend first and not a customer first you could run into problems. (Treat every friend as well as your spouses as if you are trying to satisfy a customer and you will almost never have a problem.)

Goals

Sales are nothing but a series of goals. You must start with each one and continue until you reach the final goal---closing the sale. I wanted to talk about goals a little because I see a lot of salespeople not really understanding how to achieve their sales goals or quotas. The first thing I always do when I find out what my quota or sales goal is for the month is break it down into smaller numbers. I never worry about or look at it as it is too much, I just break it down. I would take the number and divide by how many days in the month to get a daily number. Next I would take what my average deal size was and divide the number I got by the transaction size. I would then add the amount that I knew I would not close or had credit problems by looking at my past close rate to get a true number of deals that I need to do a day. Then take that number and add about 20% to it because your goal should be to exceed quota. I quickly would find out that I needed to do 27 deals a day at an average of $4000 to be able to meet my goal.

This might sound complicated but it is actually very simple. The best secret to making a quota is to determine how many deals I needed to do a day. I would not go home until I had done the 27 deals. If on any given day my average deal size went below the $4000, I did not worry as long as I did the correct number of deals. To say the least I always met and most of the time exceeded my quotas. You have to be able to crunch the number in order to better understand how your goal will come into play in your current situation.

Look back at the 10-3-1 rule. This rule is about meeting your number and breaking it down into a smaller goal. I once heard Zig Zigler talking about losing weight. He stated that he wanted to loose 40 lbs over the next year. He would take that number and divide it by 12. That is less than 1 lb a week. I know that everyone that will try can lose 1 lb a week. This is to better understand how short term goals help to meet long-term goals.

Now I mentioned several items in my quota such as close rate and average deal size. You have got to know your own numbers. You cannot set correct goals or accurate goals without knowing every trend that you have and how you do in certain situations. I had a person that I was mentoring about a year ago who had just started with us. She was having problems meeting her quotas. I showed her how to figure how many deals a day she needed to do. The first few days she met her number goal but the dollar amount was not there. I explained how it would all come out correctly because you took the number from an overall average. She is now one of the top producers in her group and continues to over exceed her number. Set your goals accordingly and you will be surprised how well you do. Finally make sure that you understand how your company and you manager measure your success. Is the quota the only thing they are interested in? Again, I measure performance by results, but this may not be the case in your manager's eyes.

Financial Plan

I want to talk about a financial plan because it took me several years to understand that commissioned sales people will not get the same amount on their checks every month. You will have to better understand how to "pay yourself first" and not get caught short every few months.

One thing that I used to do when I knew I was going to get a bigger check one month was I had a separate account that I always deposited my check into. I would then transfer money into my everyday checking account. I would "pay myself first" which was a great way to help budget and save money. A lot of new sales people do not do well with their personal budgets because when they get a smaller check they, of course, are living above their means.

Set up some kind of a financial plan in addition to your company's 401(K) or stock plan. Put a monthly amount that you will not miss into a mutual fund or an IRA. Utilize your time and the years that you intend to work to be able to help create a better future. The earlier you start the better. No amount is too small. Just do something.

I had a friend in the insurance business that would sometimes go months without a check and then get a big check for over 6 months worth of commissions. He set up a separate account and had it done as a bank draft to pay himself every 2 weeks. I thought this was one of the best ideas on budgeting that I had seen. Just remember to understand how and when you are going to get paid and how to budget your monthly expenses correctly. Don't count on a $10,000 dollar commission check if you only get one that large once a year. Get your average and then try to live below that number. You will come out okay and do fine.

Mentors

The main thing I can say about a mentor is get one or several. I told you about what I always do when I go into a new situation. I find the guy who is doing it the best and try to find out what they are doing and why they are the best. A mentor will not pick you; you will need to find a mentor. Without a mentor, I would only know a fraction of what I have discussed in this book. Look at the people who are successful around you and do what they are doing. You will be amazed how easy this is. People in general want to help, so if you ask, most of the time you will get the help you are asking for. Every person who has ever become great at something has a mentor that they look up to and try to emulate.

Now, after you achieve your goals and better understand how and why people buy or whatever professions you are in pick out a new person in the job and try to be a mentor to them. You will not only be able to help them but you will quickly find out how much you know yourself. There is no better way to help improve your own skills other than trying to teach them to someone else. Be a leader in whatever you do, you will find much more quality in life if you help others in their endeavor to become the best. To quote Zigler again "You can achieve everything you want in life by helping others achieve everything they want in life".

Chapter 6
Personal Development

Personal development is an area of interest every salesperson needs to talk about and also think about. Why did you get into sales? I know that most people see a profession in sales as a great money making opportunity. Why? Because if you are on a commission basis, and you should be, your income potential should be unlimited as far as possibilities are concerned. Take advantage of your commission structure and use it to help create a great income for yourself and your family.

J. Paul Getty was an American oil billionaire reputed to be the richest man in the world when he died in 1976 at the age of 84. He owned a controlling interest in Getty Oil Company as well as almost 200 other companies. A few of the great things about Mr. Getty are that his greatest business adventure did not come until he was almost 60 years old. He was married and divorced five times and had an idea that he wrote down about how to gain wealth. He called it the "8 rules for wealth secrets". These rules pertain to the sales industry very well and I felt compelled to share them with you. Remember he wrote these over 30 years ago.

J. Paul Getty's Wealth Secrets

Rule No. 1: To acquire wealth today, you must be in your own business.

You may think that the corporate executive with a $100,000 salary is better off than the small shop owner, but the executive will be hard-pressed to double his income and taxes will eat up most of any increase. The simplest peanut vendor has unlimited opportunity to expand his business and his income and even a salesman, who in most cases is able to write his own paychecks, can control his sale increases himself.

Rule No. 2: You must have a working knowledge of the business when you start and continue to increase your knowledge of it as you go along.

If you don't know what you're doing when you start, your mistakes will be costly and often unnecessary, and you won't be able to keep up with the technological explosions in any field. Start smart and stay that way.

Rule No. 3: You must save money in your personal life and in your business venture as well.

Discipline is the key to saving money. You must develop the will power to deny yourself immediate gratification or the temptation to gamble on the "quick buck". Resources will be needed for expansion and should be guarded carefully.

Rule No. 4: You must take risks, both with your own money and with borrowed money.

Risk taking is essential to business growth. Nelson Bunker Hunt is admired for his guts in trying to corner the silver market, not scorned for losing money on this deal. Some of the richest men have staked their entire fortunes and lost, several times over, before the risk taking paid off. Back those risks with good judgment, experience, commitment and the right support. Seek advice on risks from the wealthy who still take risks, not friends who dare nothing more than a football bet.

Rule No. 5: You must not only learn to live with tension, you must seek it out.

Thrive on stress! If it means getting physically fit, having a psychiatric overall or losing 50 pounds before you can handle it. Do it! Once you can learn to thrive on stress, you will not only enjoy it, you will seek it out willingly, enthusiastically and wonder how you could live any other way. Men of means look at making money as a game which they love to play. Consider it serious business and you will suffer far more stress than you need or want. Keep your perspective or your stress level will rocket beyond your control.

Rule No. 6: Build wealth as a by-product of your business success.

If wealth is your only objective in business, you will probably fail. Wealth is only a benefit of the game. If you win, the money will be there. If you lose, and you will from time to time – if you play long and hard enough – it must have been fun or it was not worth it.

Rule No. 7: Patience

This is the greatest business asset. Wait for the right time to make your moves. Let your business grow naturally not by pressing your luck.

Rule No. 8: Diversify at the top.

Once you've made it, you'll understand that any business is limited in the challenges it offers. You'll want and need other games to play, so you'll look for other ventures to hold your interest.

Mr. Getty's words have long been studied and they seem to withstand the test of time. I can see where you could this very day apply all these rules in your sales career. Do you think the dot-com business would have had a different outcome if these simple rules had been applied to the millions of dollars spent to start internet businesses? I feel like you would have seen a different outcome.

My dear friend, Brady Johns, and I regularly have discussions on this very subject. Brady and I grew up together and often sometimes daily have discussions on the different aspects of business. I recall a time some ten years ago when we were having a simple discussion about a balanced life. We drew a pie chart on a napkin and tried to focus on how the pie should be divided between home life, work, stress and a variety of other ideas. I tell you all this because Brady and I have traveled a lot of the same roads. We have had several common jobs as we do now. Brady is at the top of his field in just a few short years. We talked today at lunch about why and where our sales success had come from.

We came to the conclusion that sales are like anything else in life. You have to get an education in order to become good and knowledgeable at what you are doing. You have to study the game. Learn from your mistakes. I am not just talking about a college degree in your chosen field but always trying to learn from others that have come before you in the same role. I believe that Mr. Getty probably never stopped studying the successful people around him.

Just as in a formal education class you also have to fail a few classes in order to complete your education. As mentioned before I can name several top-notch people who failed many times over before they became successful. Some of my first sales calls were pure failure. I have made a lot of mistakes in my career but have always tried to learn from them. You must realize that in studying your field you may never graduate. I will continue to try new approaches and new techniques as long as I am selling. I feel like to master one subject just means it is time to move onto another subject. Be a student of the game and learn from your mentors.

Brady and I, while growing up, started taking martial arts together in a never ending quest to be as good as the late and great Bruce Lee. We would practice together and work out together. We went through the ranks and both acquired our black belts together. To this day we both consider this as one of our greatest accomplishments in our lives. The reason we were able to do this was because we became students and were not afraid to learn something new. We also made it a priority in our lives to succeed and become good at what we were learning. I tell you this to remind you that every time the door opens and you have the chance to tell your story and make a presentation you need to be prepared. As in the same way if you have the chance to see what someone else is doing and how their presentation is take advantage of this chance.

If someone comes to my door trying to sell me something I always listen. I might not purchase from them but I do listen and observe what they do and how they do it. In the last few days I had a gentleman come up to me while I was outside and make a presentation for a discount food coupon. (I listened to his presentation and although I <u>did not buy</u> from him I did let him know that the product he was offering was a <u>good one</u> and he did <u>explain the program</u> very well. I also made the note to him that although I <u>did not buy</u> one of his coupons he had a <u>strong presentation</u> as well as a <u>good product</u> and

I could tell that he would sell a lot of the coupons if he did not give up.) I have been in this young man's shoes and understand how frustrating it is to give a great pitch and still have the customer say "No". I have no doubt in my mind that the man went on to sell several coupons later that day.

As Brady and I discussed amongst ourselves there are several reasons why people fail. We believe that there are a lot more reasons why people fail than why they succeed. Again, one of the main reasons why we feel that people fail is because they have a lack of knowledge and understanding of what they are trying to accomplish.

I had a car lot that was located next to one of my stores in Corpus Christi, Texas. The owner would come into my store almost every morning and get coffee. Day after day I would listen to him tell me that he was having problems selling more than four or five cars a month. He complained that he was not making what he wanted to and asked me for my help in coming up with a solution as how he could sell more cars.

The first thing I noticed is that his lot was small and he only had six cars as his inventory. I tried to explain to him that you could not sell something that you did not have. My advice to him was to move to a bigger lot or at the least go out and get six more cars for his inventory. If he wanted to sell twelve cars a month than he really needed about fifteen or twenty cars as inventory on his lot. He thought about what we talked about for a couple of weeks. He later moved his location and tripled his inventory. To his surprise, he started to sell around eighteen cars a month and was now doing what he needed to do to stay in business.

I have mentioned Flea Markets several times because I like them. I have seen on several occasions where a vendor would spend forty dollars on a booth but only have about fifty dollars worth of inventory. Just as the car lot, if he sold everything he had, he could not have a good day of sales. (I bring this up to better understand where your sales will come from.) Is your inventory up to par? Not only physical inventory but also mental inventory, do you know where your next sale will come from? Have you studied the game?

You want to know why there are successful salespeople while others struggle? Because they are not prepared to do their job effectively as they should.

Conclusion

I have gone over almost ten years worth of learning the sales profession in the last five chapters. These things did not come by accident but by learning. If I fell down I would get right back up. You have to learn how to overcome obstacles in your life and in your career while maintaining a balance between the two.

What makes successful people successful? Here is the great secret to all sales and even to life itself; successful people do the things that unsuccessful people are unwilling to do. They do the common things uncommonly well. Successful people will create habits that failures do not. Successful people do not want to do these things any more than the failure does but he is willing to do them anyway. I do not like, actually I hate to make a cold call but if that is what will make the difference between success and failure then I will make cold calls. I do not like to keep track of calls and outbound, however, I do it on a daily basis.

It is not an accident that I learned these things but I sought it out. I have lost a lot of sales but always tried to learn from my mistakes. Being at the top of one's field has to be a desire and not just an act of hard work. I know several people that work much harder and put in more hours than I do without the same results.

Look at the presentation, the Elvis way. Create your great stage performance and present it to ten people in the hopes that three will listen and one will take to heart what you presented to them. It is all just as easy as C.A.K.E with a little bit of F.U.D mixed in. You have created a loyalty without sitting on "china eggs" while understanding that people will buy from you because they like you and they will always listen to their emotions over logic. You have overcome the objection of the customer as well as received at least three referrals from them in the process. You have gone back and checked to make sure you covered everything on the agenda while understanding through listening to what the customer has told you to better understand what color they would represent. You have identified what type of customer they are, you have set the next appointment and written your thank you letter. You have out bounded when needed and finally you have closed the sale. You asked to write the business. When you received your paycheck, you put money back and paid yourself first. You have set your goals and created your financial plan for the future. You revisited Mr. Getty's wealth secrets to better understand and check on your progress. You have become the mentor to a fellow salesperson on your team and helped to teach that person the importance of "Never Say Buy, Never Say Sell!"

Good luck in your career, happy selling and may God bless you in ways you never thought possible.

References Cited

Elvis, Elvis Presley are all part of Elvis Presley Enterprises and are in no way associated with this book. Used as a reference only and not be taken as a true system or affiliation

Rolex is a copyrighted trademark and used as example only

Dell Financial Services L.P. is part of the Dell Corporation

IBM Business Services Inc cited as example

Ralph Lauren is a trade mark and used for example only, no affiliation with this book

Mercedes Benz is a trade mark and used for example only, no affiliation with this book

Nolan Ryan, Public statistics quoted from National Baseball Hall of Fame

Dale Carnegie, cited by example

The Color Test used as public information and credit given to Taylor Hartman, PH.D

J. Paul Getty and Getty Oil, cited from J. Paul Getty's Wealth Secrets Circa 1965

About the Author

Christopher Fielder grew up in a small town north of Dallas, Texas by the name of Gainesville, population of about 16,000. He attended Tarleton State University in Stephenville, Texas on a full music scholarship. His sales career started early when he realized that if he could sell himself then he could sell anything. At the young age of 21, he started his first real sales job as an Account Executive or Road Salesman (nickname from the industry) with Caldwell Music Company, Inc. out of Abilene, Texas. As a road salesman with Caldwell he traveled West and Central Texas calling on high schools and small businesses to build a relationship for repeat business. As a music major and accomplished percussionist, he was named to the largest Drum Corporations in the world as one of 14 field clinicians. This company was the Ludwig Corporation where he performed and taught clinics to marching drum lines across the state. Christopher spent the first six years of his sales career with Caldwell as well as maintaining his relationship and clinician status with Ludwig.

After leaving Caldwell Music Company, Christopher opened his own business. He and a partner opened and operated a chain of four convenience stores in the Corpus Christi and the Dallas area specializing in tobacco and cigars. In a matter of only three years the business grew to gross sales of over two million a year. Christopher refined his sales skills by understanding the retail market as well as what small business owners can expect. The stores were sold off to his partner and to this day are still in operation.

After the role of business owner Christopher went back to his sales roots. He took a leasing and finance job with Dell Financial Services L.P., which is a captive leasing company for Dell Computer Corporation in Austin, Texas. Christopher has remained at the top of his field. With Several promotions in less than a year Christopher quickly outgrew DFS and continued his career in the leasing and finance realm as a broker for TEAM Equipment Leasing, Inc. He maintains a top sales performance through the selling aspects related to in his book. He has negotiated million dollar deals and ultimately contributes to the bottom line of the company.

TEAM Equipment Leasing, Inc is a small company where Christopher can work with his sales skills. His attitude has helped him to adjust quickly. Christopher is the Director of Sales and practices and teaches the skills and techniques found in this book. He has put together a sales team that has out performed the sales objectives and increased the bottom line by over 40% growth a year.

He shares his life with his wife, MaShon, daughter Hailey and son Christian. Christopher contributes his successful career to the support of his family and his strong Christian beliefs. He believes in an overall mix of family and work and the idea that there is life beyond the workday.

Christopher is available for speaking engagements and believes in measuring performance by results. He brings with him over fourteen years of sales and leasing experience and can enhance any sales team with his simple approach to becoming the best sales person possible.

Printed in the United States
143253LV00001B/6/A